On a dry erase board in our youngest d̶... the verse Christa had challenged our three girls to memorize: "Above all else, guard your heart, for everything you do flows from it" (Prov. 4:23). During those years she lived with us and played with Michael in his band, she profoundly impacted our children with the way she walked her faith out before them. Little did we know that some of the struggles she shared with us (and many she didn't) would eventually lead her to healing and the wise words in these pages. We urge you to read this book and open your hearts as you do ... it's a beautiful guide to the healing Jesus longs to bring to every broken piece of your heart!

—**Michael W. Smith**

If anyone can take you on a heart journey to freedom and wholeness, it is this powerful woman of God. The seat of her power is a constant Christ-centered experience of life.

I know Christa and Luke. I've witnessed indescribable agony overwhelmed by the Comforter. This book will transform you because the author is deeply authentic in Christ.

—**Graham Cooke**, Brilliantperspectives.com

Heart Made Whole is a wonderfully vivid and beautifully raw account of the journey that Christa and her family have endured. From rejection to redemption, betrayal to belonging, this book guides the wounded heart to the only place where we can experience wholeness: the Heart of the Father. This is a must-read in any season of life, and it's still impacting me.

—**Meredith Andrews**, Worship leader and
Dove Award-winning recording artist

Heart Made Whole is a stunning book that lets you look into life and its deepest of pains. Christa, the author, has lived deep pain. In this book she shares her process. How do you live life when it feels like your whole world will never be worth anything again? The beauty of this book gives you tools on how to live again and, most importantly, how to find God and let the healing happen.

—**Beni Johnson,** Author of *Healthy and Free* and *The Happy Intercessor*

Almost everyone battles feelings of hurt and loss at some point in their lives. I know I have. That's exactly why Christa Black Gifford's life-changing book *Heart Made Whole* is a must-read. It is honest, vulnerable, and brave. Christa's passion for helping other hearts be made whole is beautiful.

—**Alli Worthington,** Author of *Breaking Busy: Finding Peace and Purpose in a World of Crazy*

I am a firm believer that you cannot take others where you have not been yourself. Christa writes from a raw and real place, and I have watched as she has walked through the valley of the shadow of death and come through victoriously on the other side.

The Bible says clearly that out of our heart flows the issues of life, yet too many people are coping through life with fractured hearts and wonder why they are not living in the fullness of what Jesus promised for them. As you read these pages, apply these truths, and allow Jesus to come in and breathe life where there was death, you will discover a freedom that is life-changing. Christa's ability to articulate this process is breathtaking and inspiring. Thank you, Christa, for your transparency and vulnerability on every page and for the truth of God's Word that will bring freedom into the lives of every reader.

—**Alex Seeley,** Pastor, The Belonging Co Church, Nashville

Deep, honest, powerful, and moving, *Heart Made Whole* is a book like no other I have ever read. I was gripped by Christa's raw storytelling and changed by her leadership into the exploration of my own heart. This book took courage to write, and I'm so thankful Christa was willing.

—**Annie Downs,** Author of *Looking for Lovely* and *Let's All Be Brave*

The truth, depth, and transparency Christa has shared in *Heart Made Whole* is so impacting. I believe it will help you to overcome your pain and come to know God as the Healer, Restorer, and gracious Father He is, reminding you of a love that is present in the darkest of moments to make your heart whole.

—**Kari Jobe**

What Christa and Lucas had to go through when they lost their daughter, Goldie, is unimaginable. I wish that they never had to experience one ounce of what they did. However, I am so grateful that Christa had the ability and strength to take her broken heart to Jesus and not only learn how to navigate through the pain, but also be gracious enough to share her journey and heart lessons with all of us. It's not every day that we get invited into the deepest darkest places of someone's heart and get to watch how they triumphed through tragedy and came out victorious on the other side. Her wisdom is invaluable, and this book is a true treasure.

—**Anjelah Johnson-Reyes**

While most of us have never experienced the unimaginable pain of losing a child, we all have experienced pain in our lives. That pain, when not dealt with properly, wreaks havoc on a heart that was meant to be fully alive by experiencing the radical love of a Father. As I read *Heart Made Whole,* I was deeply affected and ministered to as Christa, through her writing, spoke truth and life into my own heart. Christa has given us an incredible gift as she opens up her life in intimate ways to reveal how even the most broken hearts can be made whole.

—**Banning Liebscher**, Founder and pastor of Jesus Culture

Christa's vulnerability and honesty on these pages is nothing short of astounding. I found myself letting the tears silently roll as my heart breathed a sigh of relief. If we let it, this book could affect the way we approach the intricacies of being human—from today forward. I know it will for me.

—**Amanda Cook**

I have had the great honor of knowing Christa for five years now. As a friend, I grieved with her when her sweet baby girl died and in the days following. I watched in amazement as God began to heal and transform her heart. In her new book *Heart Made Whole*, Christa writes with authority, passion, and incredible vulnerability. This is a book for every gender, every generation, and every heart that refuses to be bound and broken. Christa's heartfelt words and experience will inspire you!

—**Kim Walker-Smith**, Jesus Culture

This book takes you on a journey. By the first few paragraphs you are bawling, and by the end you feel a sense of inner strength that completely rocks you from the inside out. Christa doesn't just share her story, but invites you to really evaluate your own, and what I loved most was her transparency and rawness through it all. READ it, TAKE it in, and GIVE your heart the healing and wholeness it's been looking for.

—**Blanca**

HEART MADE WHOLE

HEART MADE WHOLE

TURNING YOUR UNHEALED PAIN INTO YOUR GREATEST STRENGTH

CHRISTA BLACK GIFFORD

ZONDERVAN

Heart Made Whole
Copyright © 2016 by Christa Black Gifford

Requests for information should be addressed to:
Zondervan, 3900 *Sparks Drive SE, Grand Rapids, Michigan 49546*

ISBN 978-0-310-34650-0 (ebook)

Library of Congress Cataloging-in-Publication Data

Names: Black, Christa, author.
Title: Heart made whole / Christa Black Gifford.
Description: Grand Rapids : Zondervan, 2016. | Includes bibliographical
    references and index.
Identifiers: LCCN 2015049867 | ISBN 9780310346494 (softcover : alk. paper)
Subjects: LCSH: Consolation. | Suffering--Religious aspects--Christianity. |
    Children--Death--Religious aspects--Christianity.
Classification: LCC BV4909 .B534 2016 | DDC 248.8/6--dc23 LC record available
    at http://lccn.loc.gov/2015049867

Scripture quotations marked TPT are from the following books from The Passion
Translation®: *The Psalms: Poetry on Fire; Luke and Acts: To the Lovers of God;*
and *Letters from Heaven: By the Apostle Paul.* Copyright © 2014, 2015. Used by
permission of BroadStreet Publishing Group, LLC, Racine, Wisconsin, USA. www
.thepassiontranslation.com. All rights reserved.

Other Scripture versions quoted in this book are listed on pages 199–200, which
hereby become a part of this copyright page.

Any Internet addresses (websites, blogs, etc.) and telephone numbers in this book
are offered as a resource. They are not intended in any way to be or imply an
endorsement by Zondervan, nor does Zondervan vouch for the content of these
sites and numbers for the life of this book.

Published in association with the literary agent of The Burson Agency.

Cover design: Libby Gifford
Interior design: Kait Lamphere

First Printing April 2016 / Printed in the United States of America

To my little Goldie.

When your heart stopped beating, the pain that came smashed my heart into a million pieces. But even when my heart wanted to die along with you, the Comforter and Healer became as real as breath—wrapping me up in love, restoring peace.

In your forty minutes on this earth, you taught me more about life than I've ever known.

You're my hero, baby girl, and I miss you every day.

Until my arms hold you again,
Mommy

Contents

Foreword

This book is so beautiful, so necessary. I fear my words won't do it justice. This is not merely a collection of pretty words tied up into the neat package of a book. What you hold in your hands is treasure.

Living gold.

Heart Made Whole was forged in seasons of great travail and loss. Don't read this if you want to retain your excuses. Pass it on to a friend if you want to live within the containment of faith formulas. Push it aside now if you want to avoid pain ... because it goes there.

But if you are feeling brave and ready to heal ... read on.

I met Christa on the threshold of this story. It was in a green room at a conference that we had both chosen to attend.

I loved her instantly.

She was larger than life. In my mind she was a cross between a Celt and an Amazonian warrior ... her cascading hair, a statuesque body, and the pixie twinkle in her eye brought to mind an elven princess. Christa was pregnant, but not just with child; she was pregnant with promise. Everything about her made me smile. You could not help but want to touch her ... what was in her and on her was just that vibrant. I remember praying over her, the baby, and her upcoming labor. My first labor had been hard and my second one a breeze in comparison. I wanted a breeze for Christa.

I began to watch her from afar. Something in me wanted to protect her. Christa writes music that is more than songs and books that are more than words. They are wrapped in life and breath.

Time passed. Her beautiful baby girl, Goldie, was born, but she couldn't stay.

I will never understand what Christa went through. I was not there, and even if I had been, I wouldn't understand the depths of this intimate loss. I could only watch as Christa wrote. She penned the agony of her soul and the faithfulness of her Father. I cried in my kitchen as I read her blog on social media. Her words were raw, real, honest, and ethereally beautiful. I knew then that light had pierced Christa's soul and that out of this suffering would come pure gold. This gold is not to be treated lightly ... hide it in your heart and heal.

The Old Testament has over three hundred references to gold. Some of my favorites are found in the unlikely book of Job.

Receive instruction from his mouth, and lay up his words in your heart. If you return to the Almighty you will be built up; if you remove injustice far from your tents, if you lay gold in the dust, and gold of Ophir among the stones of the torrent bed, then the Almighty will be your gold and your precious silver. For then you will delight yourself in the Almighty and lift up your face to God. (Job 22:22–26 ESV)

Thank you, Christa, for choosing to lift your face so that countless others will have the courage to find healing and strength in their places of pain. I love you, and I am so very proud of you.

—Lisa Bevere

Bestselling author of *Fight Like a Girl, Lioness Arising,* and *Kissed the Girls and Made Them Cry*

Cancer survivor

The Broken Heart

A s the muscles in my body began to tighten once again, I exhaled slowly and closed my eyes, preparing for the next wave of pain that crashed down hard with each contraction.

Noises of frantic preparation for my home birth echoed down the hall and into my parents' guest bedroom, where I perched awkwardly on the end of the bed, holding the underside of a watermelon belly that felt as if it might burst. My projected due date to meet our first daughter, Luca Gold, wasn't for two more weeks, and because I had been eleven days overdue with my son, we hadn't prepared for an early arrival.

My husband, Lucas, quickly joined my dad to rearrange the living room furniture, roll back the rug, and inflate and fill the birthing tub with warm water. We called the midwife to let her know she needed to get there as quickly as possible, and Mom ushered my almost two-year-old son Moses out the door with a friend so he wouldn't drive monster trucks over my belly during labor. As my mother returned through the front door, I could hear her voice echoing through the house: "This is just so exciting! Today is the day we get to meet our Goldie!"

Another contraction came, this time more intense than the rest, and like a bowling ball toppling to the floor, my baby girl dropped hard into my pelvis. I looked down at the white bedspread and fluffy new white carpet and decided to push myself up in between contractions to waddle into the nearest bathroom, knowing that no matter how eager my mother was to meet her granddaughter, she probably wouldn't want me giving birth on her white carpet.

The moment I reached the toilet, easing myself down, I felt a pop.

"My water broke!" I cried out all alone in the darkness, realizing that the twelve-hour labor I endured with my son might turn into a twelve-minute labor with my daughter.

I could still hear everyone running around frantically in the living room and wondered if they had even heard me shout. And though I couldn't wait to meet my little Goldie, having a baby all alone in the dark while sitting on a toilet wasn't exactly what I had envisioned in my birthing plan.

I picked up my phone on the edge of the bathtub and texted my husband quickly. "Water broke!"

Still no husband. Still no midwife.

I felt helpless against a force working to push my baby girl out while I fought desperately to hold her in.

"Babe! She's coming!" I screamed.

I stood instinctively to my feet, reaching down as my husband raced around the corner just in time to place his hands underneath mine to catch our baby girl. As we felt her soft skin for the first time, we pulled her body up in anticipation of the cries of life. Instead, we encountered a screaming silence.

Our precious Goldie was missing the top of her skull and most of her brain.

We let out a scream. The baby girl in my arms wasn't moving, and from the looks of things, we didn't know if she was even alive. Our midwife, Carol, ran in behind Luke right when Goldie emerged from my womb, and she immediately stepped in to take over, praying loudly as she tucked my daughter's little body close to my heart.

"Oh, Jesus, oh, Jesus," she whispered beneath our wails and sobs, working to clean up the disaster that should have been a celebration.

With help from all sides, I shuffled slowly back to the bedroom, my body still heavy under the weight of trauma and the shock of labor. Cradling my daughter in my arms, I crumpled in a pile of sobs onto the bed. I held her warm little body close, as though clinging to life itself, horrified by the unexpected sight of my baby girl whose eyelid had been torn back in birth, and whose underdeveloped brain was exposed. A part of me was petrified to look at the nightmare unfolding in my arms, but as a mother who could see nothing but beauty in her child, I couldn't keep my eyes off of her little face—so innocent and pure.

Luke crawled up beside us onto the bed, his usually stoic frame collapsing with grief, while Carol pulled out her tools to begin checking my body and examining Goldie for signs of life. My baby girl lay as still and stiff as a porcelain doll, but after pressing the metal stethoscope up to her tiny chest, Carol looked up into my eyes.

"I hear a heartbeat," she whispered.

Luke and I cried out in disbelief, weeping with joy that our daughter was alive, but facing the horror that at any moment our little gold bird might fly away and leave us as quickly as she had come. I didn't know what was wrong, much less if it could be fixed, and I was too afraid to ask any questions—too petrified to know what was really happening. The mother bear inside longed to fight for the life of her daughter, but looking at her condition, my mercy heart was mortified at the thought of her enduring life in this state.

As Carol continued to work, securing the umbilical cord, I wrapped my daughter's tiny hand around my finger and kissed her soft lips over and over, a waterfall of tears running down my chin onto her perfect skin. Every few minutes, Carol would stop and check her heart again and we would hold our breath each time.

"She still has a heartbeat. Do you want to hear?"

Luke reached eagerly for the stethoscope and placed it to his ears, caressing her perfect face while listening to the miracle of life that flowed through her veins.

For the next forty minutes, our little Luca Gold's heart fought to beat on this earth. She was so brave and so strong, fighting to be with her family for as long as she could. Within those precious minutes, we kissed her little face, her hands, and her open wounds. We prayed, embraced, and wept. We wrapped her up in something pretty and soft and took picture after picture, longing to never forget what time would soon run past. Every moment was stabbed with excruciating pain, yet every time her heart beat, our hearts pounded with irrational hope.

But her little body wasn't whole enough to let her soul remain. As brief as a breath on the wind, our Goldie was gone.

We sat numbed from shock, our bodies fighting for breath, knowing our daughter would never breathe again.

As Luke crawled off the bed to stand beside me, I watched his strong arms fall down helplessly, unable to protect and fix the way he always could. Whispering in between sobs, I reached out for his hand.

"Babe, do you want to hold her?"

My husband reached out to cradle the lifeless body of his only daughter and lift her into his arms—the little girl he had dreamed of fighting for, adoring with kisses and songs, and someday walking down the aisle. As if he was hit by a truck, his knees buckled as his body crashed into the wall, sliding down to crumple into a heap of tears onto the floor.

I lay in bed, head swirling, watching the surreal scene unfolding beside me. Every part of my physical body still ached from the pain of natural childbirth, but that pain felt like a paper cut compared to the torturous agony that had just detonated within my heart. It was as if a nuclear bomb had been dropped and my insides were exploding into pieces while I sat and watched. The world was spinning so quickly that every cell of my body fought to cling to some sort of reality, but the anguish was so tormenting that a part of my heart just wanted to give up and die with my daughter.

I closed my eyes and let the precious gift of air fill my

lungs—a gift I took for granted each day. If I didn't stop the spin and hold on tightly to something—anything—I knew that I could easily get lost in the blast. In this moment—the worst moment of my life—I could allow the inferno of pain to burn at my heart, destroying my soul with bitterness, rage, and distrust. I could put up a fortress inside in my fury against betrayal. I could shake my fist at heaven and point my finger in accusation, putting God on trial for abandoning my daughter as her lifeless body lay in my husband's arms.

But I had learned from years of dealing with heart-pain incorrectly—through trying to hide it, numb it, or avoid it—that pain never goes away on its own. It must be felt, embraced, and brought to a Healer. I knew that these were the kinds of moments that wrote the pages of the future. This kind of trauma was powerful enough to ruin my marriage. It was heavy enough to dam up my joy, forever damaging my young son and future children. I knew from experience that this kind of tragedy can turn a heart into stone, eventually shutting it down completely in order to survive. It was strong enough to spin me back into addictions, depression, performance, and all the cages I had fought so hard to climb out of over the years. I knew that in these seconds of extreme torture, the choices I made would affect my heart, my relationships, and the rest of my days on planet earth.

I sighed deeply through the sobs and reached up, placing my hand over my heart—the same heart smashed to pieces by the violent hand of tragic death. Inside of my broken heart, I made the choice that changed my life.

I chose to take my pain to Jesus.

UNAVOIDABLE PAIN

I hope you will never know the hell on earth of burying a baby girl as I did, but if you're breathing right now, then I guarantee that you have had all sorts of awful experiences that crashed at your heart like a wrecking ball operated by a cruel world. As long as we live in a fallen world where sin, death, and time exist, trouble and pain will visit us all.

Moreover, adversity doesn't just come in big packages like death—it can be small, annoying, and wrapped up so ugly, you'd rather just send it back. There were times in my past when being unable to fit into my jeans was on par with the end of the world, and other times when getting stuck in a traffic jam warranted the annihilation of my fingernails. Canceled flights have left me stranded, and boys have left me abandoned. I have found my bank account overdrawn, survived multiple car wrecks, and had more than my fair share of backstabbing betrayals. I've dealt with the ravages of addiction, suffered the scars of sexual abuse, and landed in rehab from an eating disorder—all while living in an abundant first-world country with the rarity of loving, Christian, middle-class parents who are still happily married.

Although my early days bloomed with an abundance of good more than bad, the nature of the bad experiences early on ate away at my heart, and I limped like a cripple into my adult years. The longer the traumas of life went unhealed, the more the pain poisoned every moment, eventually plaguing my life with the diseases of depression and addiction. Days turned upside down into constant night, and joy became a land I wasn't sure I would ever visit again. At many points, it felt easier to just stop breathing and end it all.

As I have learned over years of traveling, meeting thousands of people, suffering doesn't discriminate according to age, gender, race, social class, or even Christian or non-Christian—even though most of us in the Jesus camp would like for it to. For years, I subconsciously assumed that as a follower of Christ, I had somehow received an exemption pass to be carried over the horrendous trials of life. I truly believed that being a Christian assured me that tornados would never hit my house, that murderers wouldn't choose to kill me, and that I'd never have any major physical or financial problems as long as I believed in the power of God, declaring His promises in my life. But when trouble kept smacking me out of left field, my betrayed heart always blamed the same God for not doing His promised job to protect me as His little girl. Deep down, I assumed that He kept breaking His word and dropping His sovereignty ball, reneging on His responsibility to make sure I never fell down and got hurt too badly.

But to our Christian dismay, Jesus didn't say *if* we have difficulties; He said *when*. He didn't say that if you're a faithful intercessor, all your prayers will be answered the way you want, and if you're an avid churchgoer and dedicated Bible reader, then you're assured of perpetual success. He didn't say if you're a good friend you will never be betrayed, or promise that if you're a powerful apostle, you won't be brutally murdered. Rather, Jesus promised that as long as we live in a fallen world—which we do—we will go through all sorts of adversity, even while believing in the promises of

God. I'm sure the beheaded apostle Paul, the stoned Stephen, and the crucified upside-down Peter are nodding their heavenly heads in agreement.

None of us finds out what we're made of when everything is rolling along nicely; we find out who we really are when hell is pressing in from all sides. Trauma burns with such a hot fire that if we have any cracks in our foundation, all of them will be exposed.

THE REAL ESTATE OF YOUR HEART

Each of us has an inner realm that either thrives or withers, depending on the tenants we allow to reside within. Take a moment and use your vivid imagination, seeing your heart as a large building—floor after floor built each year as life expands upward.

Your heart was dreamed up by the Master Architect before your little life ever took form, and God designed it with great attention to detail, equipping your heart with certain desires and abilities to fulfill a unique destiny. God created some of your hearts as business offices, and you find it easy to negotiate with numbers and strategy. Some are stunning art galleries, coming alive while displaying beauty, music, fashion, and creativity. Many are dripping with relational nurture, designed to be a home where life, children, ministry, and activity thrive. Others are hospitals, and you've always longed to help others, learning the human body, science, and composition. God dreamed up, fashioned, and crafted you with specific characteristics, and when you're living out your original design, the entire building pulses with life.

More often than not, however, our "buildings" sustain damage in a world where sin and death still exist. Your childhood formed the bottom of your structure, and unfortunately, many of you didn't get off to a great foundational start. If you were neglected and abused, or abandoned and mistreated, the building of your heart might have been lonely and bare, erected with dodgy, half-finished rooms trashed by tenants named pain, fear, shame, and anger. Even if your family resembled *The Brady Bunch*, none of us had a perfect childhood, and every person on earth has endured some sort of internal damage. As each year added a new layer to the real estate of your heart, at times it was easy to forget about the damaged childhood floors at the bottom the higher you climbed. But the problem is, if the bottom of your building was shaky, then it was difficult to build upward without putting the whole thing at risk for collapse.

When I was a kid, none of the boys in my class ever looked my way, even though I desperately wanted them to. And as the trauma of rejection happened over and over again throughout the years, I rented out more and more real estate in my heart to the tenant of fear—petrified that every guy in the world would find me as repulsive as the little boys of my childhood.

The thing about this kind of pain is, it doesn't stay locked away in rooms down below. It can turn into a monster gang that takes over the whole building. One little monster of rejection from childhood, after feasting for decades, can turn into Godzilla. It keeps breeding, moving into new apartments as space becomes available, to do more damage. And one tiny monster of shame can grow into a T. rex over the years—especially when your heart continues to feed the beast.

The hardest thing about my inner monster, Pain, was that as long as he was coexisting with me, his high-maintenance tendencies prevented me from enjoying my life. Because I had to focus on him all the time, afraid that I wouldn't be able to keep him hidden and appeased, I lived in constant fear and anxiety. I couldn't turn around and focus on friendships without him interfering and messing things up, or plan out my future without his fearful input and lies. He loved rearing his head at the most inopportune times to sabotage romantic love, letting me know I wasn't worthy of things like that. If a boy started coming around and getting too close, I'd make sure to act so crazy that he'd end up running for the hills. My enemy Pain would play old movies in my mind to remind me of my dirty past, my constant rejection, and current struggles—jeering in contempt when I would burst into tears.

Many times, when I had finally had enough of Pain's ruthless antics, I would grab the keys to my heart back from his hands, serving him an angry eviction notice to vacate the premises. But every time, he'd just laugh. "What are you going to do without me, Christa?" his voice would hiss and sneer, pointing at the damaged heart he had trashed and destroyed over years of abusive habitation. "I'm the only one who would ever live in this dump. And if I'm not here, you'll be all alone; even God wouldn't set foot in this filthy, sinful hole until you clean it up. But fixing yourself hasn't ever worked, has it? You might as well get used to me being around, because you're never going to change, and I'm not ever going to leave."

This Pain monster had lived with me for such a long time, I couldn't distinguish his voice from my own voice, his lies from my truth, and his heart from my heart. We had become so twisted into oneness that the tangled mess seemed more overwhelming to unravel than learning how to fly into space. I hated this monster and I didn't want him around, but without any strength to keep fighting, my only choice was to surrender and try to cope with him being there. I had resigned myself to the fact that existence was synonymous with pain, and I needed to learn how to manage this reality in order to survive. As my heart succumbed to despair, the monster named Pain would throw his scaly arm around my shoulder and once again snatch the keys out of my hands back into his own.

"Don't worry, Christa," he'd whisper into the darkness with an evil grin. "I'll take good care of you. Get used to this life, sweetie, because there's no cure for me."

As long as the monster named Pain held the keys to my heart, he was in charge of the real estate inside. And the one thing I really wanted was the one thing I believed I could never have: freedom.

If you have old, unwanted heart tenants that you have never learned to evict, I promise you: they are not going to leave your building on their own. Even though they're just renters on your property, if they're living inside, then you've allowed them to sign a lease agreement until you kick them out.

The good news is, no matter how shaky your heart foundation might be, every person is wired up for electricity at birth. When God fashioned and created you, He wired Himself into the framework of your being, hoping you would someday give Him permission to hook your power source up to His. And as Jesus knocked on your front door with salvation and you invited Him into your building, the Holy Spirit was like a worker from the electric company, plugging you into His eternal outlet of power. Because of His abiding presence inside, your entire heart will forever be capable of lighting up with new life.

But just because your electricity is turned on doesn't mean the entire building uses it. And just because Jesus and His power are always available doesn't mean every part of your heart wants to turn on the light switch—especially when old pain likes to stay hidden.

In the case of my own heart, I found that nasty tenants like fear, shame, bitterness, and anger enjoyed hiding out in dark rooms, boarding up their windows and locking doors to stay concealed. Some of my childhood trauma had been so painful, it preferred being vaulted away and forgotten as lost memories to protect me. A few of my years had been so emotionally crippling, I had built walls around entire sections of my heart.

HEART CHECK

Take a moment and place your hand on your chest, breathing in deeply and becoming aware of the physical organ that beats inside to pump life and blood to every part of your body. The blood that's pumped to your brain allows you to think and make decisions and causes the rest of your body to function. The blood pumped to your fingers and toes makes them able to move, run, work, and play. The blood pumping through your organs makes them work together to maintain life. If blood is cut off from any part of the body, that part dies. Without a healthy physical heart, your body cannot survive, and life ceases to exist.

The same is true for this metaphysical heart governing from the inside. This inner realm—the center of your being—is the origin of every move you make, every word you speak, every thought you think, and every action you take. Plainly put, your insides produce your outsides. You are the landlord of your heart, and you control who takes up residence. When God moved into your life, you didn't sign over ownership papers to your building where He took control. Rather, He gave you possession of your heart long ago and will never take back that gift. He will always be the leasing tenant, defaulting to your choices, and you will always own the property. You can choose to let Him rent out the entire building (and that is our ultimate goal as believers), but as long as you're harboring old wounds, beliefs, unforgiveness, and lies—allowing them to make themselves at home in your heart—Jesus won't bust in and kick them out. He needs your permission. He needs your master key. He needs you to give Him access to every floor, every room, and every locked, forgotten space.

For many years I didn't understand this, wanting God to just barge in and take over my heart while I lifted my hands in a worship service, putting me on autopilot. I expected myself to be perfect, or imperfect—I was either sinless or a complete fraud. I didn't understand that the gift of grace was like a lifetime warranty that covered the process of my heart transformation, empowering me to live differently. I didn't acknowledge that my heart had taken decades to break and that it might take some intentionality to heal. I didn't realize that God's whole purpose for moving into my mess was to ensure that my heart was renovated properly, room by room and floor by floor. God has never been overwhelmed by the amount of work that needs to be done inside my building or condemned me for how trashed it became over the years. In fact, He knew I didn't have the tools, knowledge, strength, or power to make everything new the way He did—which is why He chose to make my heart *His* home.

As I have walked the hard road towards my own healing, I have found that heart transformation is never about finishing a perfect building, then sitting back and relaxing for the rest of my life. It's about living in relationship with the God who resides within—learning how to surrender more inner space and lease to Him all the real estate that my heart has to offer. The apostle Paul sums it up beautifully: "This entire building is under construction and is continually growing under His supervision until it rises up, completed as the holy temple of the Lord himself. This means that God is transforming each one of you into the Holy of Holies, His dwelling place through the power of the Holy Spirit living in you" (Ephesians 2:21–22).

The problem is, because we will continue to live in a world where unexpected tornados will destroy, where wounded people keep wounding us, and where the enemy has his wrecking ball aimed at crumbling our hearts to the ground, we will always need a handy repairman as life takes its toll. Thankfully, we have continual access to a brilliant Carpenter, a Master Architect, and a General Contractor with an arsenal of power tools, ready to repair, restore, and renew everything.

PAIN CAN BE HEALED

You can't control the storms that pound against the walls of your inner realm, but you can control whether or not your heart chooses to become a shelter of peace during those storms. You can't control your parents' decision to divorce, but you can choose whether or not your heart grows bitter and cold. You can't control that you don't have a job, but you can choose whether or not you move into anxiety or stay steady with trust. You can't control the betrayal of a spouse, but your heart can choose to forgive. The space inside of your heart is the only place where you will ever have full ownership and authority. You are the guardian of your heart, and as the final say over your inner realm, you're the only one who can decide what happens next.

At this very moment, your life is the sum total of all the choices you have made, because you're the only one who can make them. You can either choose to surrender your heart to pain monsters, or to a Healer who died to make everything whole.

As I sit in a coffee shop writing these pages just five months after losing my daughter to a condition I didn't even know existed, called anencephaly, I have already had three people stop by my table and ask with genuine concern, "How are you really doing, Christa?"

When people have asked me this, most of them expect me to lie, rambling off the cliché answer, "Oh, I'm fine," to try to avoid an awkward moment. Some might think I will clam up and change the subject, or possibly even burst into tears. And when the uncontrollable tears do flow from time to time, I'm never ashamed of them. But today, and every day since my Luca Gold left my life to head home and be with Jesus, when asked this question, a part of my heart has been able to answer in a remarkable way that I never thought possible.

"Today is the most painful day of my life, but my heart is still thriving."

UNSHAKEABLE

Some might think I'm being irreverent after tragically losing my daughter. It's assumed that having feelings of true peace and even joy in the fire must mean I've cloaked myself in some sort of self-protective denial in order to survive. But I have learned the hard way that pain doesn't just go away, even when you turn your back on it.

This time around, with this level of heartache over losing my daughter, I've been determined to try a new approach.

I have chosen to turn around and run towards the pain. Like a young boy named David facing an enormous giant, I have chosen to take on the monster named Pain. I have thrown my arms around this current suffering and all the hardships that come with it and have made a commitment to feel everything as the heavy emotions of grief, anger, hurt, and loss steamroll over my soul on a daily basis. I have pledged to learn everything I can inside this fire to equip me to overcome future flames. I have invited the refining nature of extreme heat to consume everything in my heart that keeps me broken.

I have not shut down like I have in the past.

I have not medicated through addiction.

I have refused to live numb.

I have not run to escape.

And I will never turn my back on the pain of losing my daughter. She deserves better than that.

In this very moment, I'm standing inside the most agonizing moments of my life, knowing that if I don't continue to deal with the pain that accompanies this trauma, it will destroy my heart and cripple me for years to come. So each day I choose to confront the reality that I will never hear my daughter's sweet little voice, or watch her crawl for the first time, or drop her off at school and wave good-bye, or feel her soft dark curls between my fingers as she falls asleep, nestled safely under my chin. And when I sit down in the hottest fire of my life, the unexpected happens: The very place of my deepest pain miraculously becomes the starting point of my heart's greatest healing.

You see, pain itself is not the enemy. Pain is inevitable in this bumper-car life where you will continue to collide with a fallen world that you cannot control. *Unhealed* pain, however, will become your greatest foe if your broken heart is not made whole again after each collision. And dearest friend, there is only *One* who can take the shattered pieces of your heart and put it back together so that it flourishes even in the worst situations.

As I've learned from my incredible therapist mother, when you're living in wholeness with Jesus and your heart is thriving, you can be unshakeable, living fully alive in each moment, taking risks, trusting your heart, fully aware of what you love, remaining yourself in every circumstance, and adoring God with every part of your being. However, if your heart remains broken, even as a Christian you will experience consistent separation between your heart, soul, mind, and spirit that keeps you from living in joyful connection with God and others.

After years of living as a Christian with a broken, bleeding heart that continued to spew out all sorts of unpleasant things, I finally uncovered a mine of precious jewels that seemed too good to be true, but actually was true. And it began with a Holy Spirit–guided journey to the center of my truest self—the heart that Jesus loved so much that He died to live inside of it. I realized that in order to find out what it meant to live each moment from my inheritance of wholeness, I needed to learn how to let the Healer make me whole. And in order to do that, I had to let Him have full access to every emotion, every trauma and shameful truth.

I couldn't hide my wounded heart and expect it to heal. I couldn't neglect my feelings and expect them to change. I had to surrender, hold tightly to the hand of my Savior, and turn around to face the overwhelming mess. I had to allow Love to start pouring into my inner self to cast out all my fear—turning my heart into the home it was created to be.

I hope you will accompany me on a journey to the center of your truest self—letting the Light of heaven shine inside every forgotten room, condemned vault, and shameful hallway. As you allow the divine presence of Love to bind up your wounds, He will show you how to tend to your heart gently and carefully, extending kindness, patience, and mercy as it's cleansed and healed. But most of all, He will teach you how to love your heart the way He does—lavishly, fiercely, and passionately.

It's time for every part of your heart to be loved into wholeness.

Open-Heart Surgery

1. Until Jesus comes back again, trouble will be a reality in our lives. Have you lived to avoid pain and hardship, or been angry at God when life gets tough? What kinds of emotional, physical, and spiritual damage has your heart endured over the years that hasn't seemed to heal?

2. Take a few moments and meditate on the real estate of your heart. What does your "building" look like? Does it have a spotless exterior to hide the pain monsters living on the inside? Is it crumbling and broken, or strong and

whole? If you have pain monsters, what are your primary tenants? (Examples: fear, shame, bitterness, self-hatred, jealousy.)

3. Has the foundation of your heart building been shaky since childhood, affecting your adult years? Have you turned on the light in each room in your heart, allowing the light of heaven access to every part of your heart— the good and the bad? Take several minutes to write a description of your building, allowing yourself to be brutally honest with how your building makes you feel.

4. After putting your hand on your physical heart, feeling the blood pumping inside, were you able to dial into your metaphysical heart? What did it feel like? If this was hard, don't worry—most people have shut down their hearts to some extent in order to survive pain. Take a few more moments and close your eyes, breathing in deeply to become aware of your inner realm, asking the Holy Spirit to fill you. See your heart wired up for electricity, ready to come alive with the light of God. If you're tired of the pain and ready to turn on the light switch, then close your eyes and form a mental picture of the master key of your heart that gives access to all rooms inside. Hand over your key to Jesus, giving Him permission to go wherever He needs to go in the days and weeks ahead.

5. In a busy world that doesn't slow down, it's easy to focus on everyone but ourselves—especially when we don't think we're worth it. But what we need to realize is, the investment that we make in ourselves will determine

everything about our lives, making it the most important decision we could ever make. Write out a commitment letter to yourself, pledging to be honest and open as you journey to the center of your heart with the guidance and comfort of the Holy Spirit. Commit to the process, no matter how hard, long, or messy it gets. Sign and date your pledge below.

Chapter 2

Managing Trauma

The days following Luca's death crept along at a snail's pace. It felt as though grief had a tangible weight attached to it, as heavy as an elephant, threatening to flatten my fragile heart every moment.

Although I had been living in freedom for many years from all the old ways I used to medicate pain, my brain still had those memories stored and filed away. I remembered that if I binged on food, my heart would temporarily feel full and in control—and I needed to feel in control. I knew that if I drank too much whiskey at 9:00 a.m., I could pass out and forget about the pain—and I just wanted to forget. The pain was so great that I easily considered all of my old means of escape. Temptation banged on the door of my heart louder than it had in over a decade, begging to let substances back in to do their temporary job of numbing a heart screaming in unfathomable agony.

What made it worse were the well-meaning but theologically inaccurate comments and advice dispensed by fellow believers.

—"God takes the best ones to be His angels, which is why He took Goldie."

—"God knew how many people would be healed and saved because of her death, so it's why He chose her, Honey."

—"God took her from you because He knew you could handle it."

—While crying at Luca's memorial service: "God has commanded you to be of good cheer. You can grieve later."

—And my personal favorite: "I totally know how you feel. My cat just died."

Most people don't have a good understanding of trauma. All they know is that it's a bad thing that they have tried to avoid as much as possible. But even with the best efforts to steer clear of the collisions of life, sometimes trauma is as unavoidable as encountering the night.

Traumas are wounds left inside our hearts that keep us from living in wholeness. They barricade us from growth; they slow down our maturity and keep the broken fragments of our hearts from healing. When traumatic circumstances hit our hearts and we stay crushed, part of the heart can get hooked and stuck in the past, perpetuating pain and fear.

You see, the enemy might be defeated, but he sure doesn't act like it—and he's anything but stupid. He put a target on your head when you were a kid, knowing that wrecking balls of trauma could smash gaping holes within your heart, allowing pain monsters to rush inside through the unhealed wounds and burrow deep inside. Through imbedded pain monsters, you could be defined by distrust, anger, hurt, abandonment, rejection, and deep hopelessness, building your life on top of a shaky foundation of broken-ness, instead of a sure foundation of wholeness. The enemy knew that if pain lived inside your heart for long enough, it would end up controlling and ruining the abundant life God intended for you.

Plainly put, *trauma is any place in your heart where your pain stays greater than your joy.* Which means, even those set up for success in the life department have, at some point, endured trauma while living in close proximity to wounded people. The problem isn't that trauma happens, but that most of us have no idea how to repair it when part of our building remains structurally damaged.

GETTING UNSTUCK

Several years ago, as an almost newlywed who had been working as a professional musician, I landed a gig impossible to refuse—even though it meant packing a couple of suit-cases and my instruments for nine solid months away from home. Some nights our large operation was jetting between countries, surviving on precious minutes of sleep. Other times, we crawled into bunk beds on tour buses while trav-eling through the night to our next show.

Once the fleet of 18-wheelers and buses had pulled away from the venue and we were on the road, the band members on my bus would pick up their after-show meal, then migrate to the back lounge and close the door—wanting nothing to do with little ole me. For several nights I sat by myself in an empty front lounge, wiping tears that streamed down my face and feeling sorry for myself because apparently middle school had chased me into my thirties. The pain of rejection that had poured into my heart through the abandonment of my band mates had struck a lightning rod of unhealed rejection deep inside. When this new pain was combined with what was already in there, unfortunately it created an explosive agent that spewed out with all sorts of bad behaviors as we traveled the world.

The first night, while sitting alone in the front lounge of that fancy tour bus, I poured myself a glass of wine (or three) to try and medicate the hurt. And though alcohol helped to temporarily numb the rejection, the next morning as I sat at breakfast all alone, reality poured onto the top of my head like a pot of boiling water. The next day, I tried the over-compensation approach, attempting to kiss up to my bullies, adopt their language and character instead of my own, and somehow convince them that they had made a wrong decision to discard me as a friend. But my phony behaviors didn't make me look as cool as I'd hoped—they just made me look desperate and drove everyone away even faster.

Finally, when all of my scheming had failed miserably, my tone grew unusually cold, my fists were constantly clenched, and for a while I pouted around like a wounded schoolgirl on the playground who hadn't been picked for kickball. A piece of my heart was still stuck in that adolescent state, and I felt like a child being made fun of by the popular crowd because a part of my soul was still crippled from the cruelty of kids from my past.

The rejection of my peers as a thirty-year-old adult didn't feel like an isolated experience. It felt like the end of the world—because I had never dealt with the years of childhood rejection still piling high within my heart. When the trauma of my band mates' abandonment and rejection combined with the years of unhealed pain already inside, I wasn't just dealing with the emotions of an adult. I was dealing with every unhealed, rejected emotion that I'd ever experienced.

After a few months of playing the victim on that tour, trying to become cool enough for the band mates who continued to avoid me, I decided one night to stop feeling sorry for myself and ask God what He thought about the situation. To my amazement, He wasn't nearly as interested in getting everyone to like me as much as He wanted to be invited into the problem, be the solution, dig up some of the old lies within the foundation of my heart, heal me, and then make something good out of the ordeal.

One lonely night as all my band mates went out to party in Amsterdam, I sat by myself in a dimly lit Thai restaurant with red walls, and my weary heart finally said yes to the God who had been patiently waiting. My Father began flooding the supernatural medicine of His presence into my broken heart while I shamelessly sobbed over a greasy plate of Pad Thai. When I simply said yes, I gave Him my permission to begin pouring out grace as thick as golden honey, sticky and sweet, which seeped into the deepest cracks of my heart. Over the days and weeks that followed, we began to meet together inside the most unlikely place—the trashed rooms inside my heart that I had worked so desperately to hide from Him. As He uncovered the mess, saw everything, kissed my wounds, and held me close, the supernatural process of heart restoration began to heal years of rejection that had destroyed my life for decades.

Months later on that tour, as the band still cleared the front lounge to avoid my company and head to the back of the tour bus, a new, different Christa opened her computer one evening and began to write about her heart renovation. I wrote about my brokenness, my old wounds, and how God was beginning to heal places that I thought were impossible to change. I started a blog and would have been happy if I'd had a hundred followers, but after 30,000 hits in the first month, the rejection that had come to destroy me had instead been surrendered to a big God who lived inside. Pure life started flowing all over the world through the words I was writing.

Day after day, as God continued to heal my deepest pain with the enormity of His presence, the blog that poured out on that tour turned into my first book, *God Loves Ugly*. Years later, my passport is filled, and I'm still traveling the world, but instead of playing music and backing up other artists, I have the great privilege of speaking, writing, and teaching anyone who will listen as to how to break negative cycles by stepping into the intimacy, grace, and freedom that I'm still learning how to experience on a daily basis. When traumatic circumstances do hit me these days, I've learned that the faster I can run my wounds to Jesus, the faster I get "unstuck" and find healing.

The same can be true for you.

TWO KINDS OF TRAUMA

Dr. Jim Wilder, neuroscientist and coauthor of *The Life Model*,* writes that there are two types of trauma that can occur within our hearts and keep us stuck in the past: *Trauma A* and *Trauma B.*

Trauma B involves all the things that happened that never should have—like giving birth to a baby without a skull who dies while you watch. Or like physical, verbal, and sexual abuse, or bullying, abandonment, and tragic loss. It includes things such as wars, starvation, illness, rape, wrecks, discrimination, and divorce—just to name a few of the biggies.

There are all sorts of social, religious, and economic factors that cause Trauma B for some more than others, especially children who don't get a choice in the family department. But because bad things continue to happen every day throughout the world, our hearts can find us victimized by Trauma B pain that we didn't choose.

And then there's Trauma A.

As a human race created to thrive in life-giving relationships, Trauma A is the *absence* of all the things you should have received, but didn't. You needed nurture, but maybe you didn't receive enough. You needed affirmation, but perhaps you were put down instead. You longed for love and affection, but kept finding yourself wounded by rejection. And even for those of us who had attentive parents who did a fantastic job in the parental department, at the end of the

---

*E. James Wilder, Ph.D., in James G. Friesen et al., *The Life Model: Living from the Heart Jesus Gave You* (East Peoria, IL: Shepherd's House, Inc., 2004).

day no caretaker was ever able to give the perfect amount of nurture, affection, and love that the human heart needs to stay unscathed.

Because I'm a woman in ministry who talks very openly about the process of her own healing, I have received countless emails from people who can't figure out why they're struggling. They have carefully let God help them comb through their history, letting me know that they weren't abused and weren't orphaned, and many of them grew up in good families, as I did, with parents who loved on them lavishly. They weren't impoverished, weren't abandoned, and weren't malnourished. But for some reason, they find that there still seems to be structural damage in the heart that keeps attracting cycles of insecurity, anger, depression, fear, addiction, rejection, and self-hatred.

That's when I remind them: The *absence* characteristic of Trauma A can be just as painful to the heart as the abusive punches of Trauma B.

Victims severely wounded by Trauma B might initially disagree that Trauma A can be just as damaging, but a hammer feels like a hammer no matter where the blows come from. Failing to receive enough nurture, affection, and love can be just as damaging as abuse, betrayal, loss, and abandonment. Because even the best parents had less-than-perfect days—displaying moments of anger, sadness, anxiety, insecurity, and fear—they passed on their experience to whoever happened to be around—which was you. At some point in your life, whether your family had a white picket fence or your parents were drug addicts, there were times when you didn't receive what you needed to thrive as a human being. And those experiences were always painful for a heart that was created for love.

In my early twenties, when I was in treatment for an eating disorder, the rehab facility didn't separate those violently abused by satanic cults from the preachers' wives who felt alone and forgotten. They didn't place those who had been orphaned in another building separate from those who felt abandoned by wealthy parents when shipped off to boarding school. We all ended up in the same rehab center because we had tried, very unsuccessfully, to use food as a way to numb our shattered hearts—even though each of us had been hit by something entirely different. Both Trauma A and Trauma B produced pain, and when pain had gone unhealed, it kept ruining all of our lives.

SURVIVAL STRATEGIES

The unfathomable pain that accompanied my childhood trauma crushed the house of my heart, leaving gaping holes as big as the sun. Because I didn't have a clue how to deal with the aftermath, my heart made a subconscious decision to bury the pain so I could keep on living. The control center of my heart never wanted to harm me—in fact, its purpose was to keep me safe and alive. As a little girl carrying around pain as heavy as an elephant, my heart would have overloaded like a blown circuit if I had been forced to experience those debilitating emotions of abuse every minute of the day. So it did what it had to do, flipping an internal switch and compartmentalizing those feelings, guarding the pain down deep so I could keep functioning as a kid. For me to have fun playing with toys and laughing with friends, to carelessly enjoy summer breaks, ride my bike, and be a good student, I had to go into denial about the piercing wounds of abuse.

Although it was never God's will for the fall of man to happen, resulting in my early traumas, He knew that Adam and Eve would eat of the tree, resulting in sin and death released on the earth. Out of His overwhelming love for me—for all of us as His children—God brilliantly fashioned our hearts in a way that equips us to survive in the world, giving them the ability to keep pain from overwhelming us so we can function.

However, this coping mechanism was given as a *temporary* solution to help survive emotional pain, but never as God's *permanent* solution to heal it.

When pain monsters continue to feast on your broken heart, you will move from a place of thriving into an existence of surviving. You might be able to carry a load of pain monsters around as long as you have youthful strength, but eventually, just as our bodies grow weak and tired with time and age, your heart will weaken under their control. Some call the resulting explosion a midlife crisis. Some call it a nervous breakdown. Mine was called an unexpected trip to rehab. But whatever name you slap on it, pain that isn't dealt with will eventually require your immediate attention. And pretending that the monsters aren't there only means you have to deal with them later—after they've grown stronger with time.

When we say yes to Jesus at salvation, we invite His presence into every part—especially the places crippled by old hurts. God bursts into our humanity with redemption, adoption, and deliverance—equipping us with everything we need to triumph over the trauma of the past. He secured our relationship with Him by fusing us together into eternal union.

The problem is, even with this miraculous union our hearts aren't instantly zapped into maturity and perfection. They remember everything about the past and still have a tendency to hold on. We may wish that pain monsters would simply melt away the way Dorothy melted the Wicked Witch of the West with a bucket of water. But sometimes they must be approached carefully, skillfully, and with great intentionality. After salvation transforms us into new creations, sometimes the brokenness, damage, and lies from old pain monsters need to be untwisted, kicked out, and then healed through relationship with a perfect love.

But this eviction of pain monsters from our hearts doesn't just happen on its own. It requires someone much stronger than we are to usher our monsters out the door. In order to get free from the monsters that live inside, there are a few helpful things to know before serving them an eviction notice. We must understand the condition of the heart, the function of the heart, the keeper of the heart, and the purpose of the heart. And there's no better place to find those answers than to ask the Guy who created our hearts in the first place.

WHAT'S GOING ON IN THERE?

If you ask most people what's going on in their heart, they look at you as if you just asked them to unveil the contents of a secret vault they have guarded through lockdown. Sometimes they cock their head to the side with concern, as if you have given orders for a soldier to venture alone across enemy lines—without a weapon. Because many of us have seen our heart as an adversary that can sabotage our best efforts to become the person we want to be, if we're honest, we're petrified of spelunking down with Jesus and finding out what's really going on in there. But if we are ever going to fully understand ourselves and find wholeness, we have to try to find out what's inside and why God has given us hearts in the first place.

For many years, I was afraid of unzipping my chest and taking a good look down into my heart because I saw it as a confusing enemy, always working against me. Without warning, it would rise up with nasty traits like insecurity, anxiety, jealousy, and anger. Now I realize that what I was afraid of when I looked inside wasn't really a fear of my true self but a fear of seeing what the meat-grinder of pain had done to my heart over the years. Dealing with the swirling emotions that accompanied childhood trauma, I didn't have a clue how to begin healing a heart that had been beaten up by shame, rejection, inadequacy, fear, anxiety, and all the monsters that tagged along with them. No matter how hard I prayed, served, fasted, and cried out to God, I simply wasn't able to withstand the power of the pain monster inside—even as a dedicated believer who genuinely adored

God. So I did what the best of us do: I picked myself up and attempted to walk through life carrying the extra weight.

For decades I had lived submerged in a Christian culture that did a great job of teaching me about God and who I needed to be for Him. External factors, like sinless behaviors, worship, service, pure actions, and prayer were always the primary focus of a devoted life, and I was a production factory of great deeds, good works, ministry, and Christian duties. To show my dedication and love for Jesus, I would crawl up on the judgment seat of my life each day and pronounce a verdict according to what I saw, demanding change and striving to improve things that I thought were lacking or broken. Rarely did I even attempt to understand the design of my God-given heart. I didn't see it as a friend; in fact, I actually hated my heart for being so wounded that it sabotaged my life.

Through all sorts of unwanted childhood experiences, the enemy had devised a strategy to destroy me—making sure that my heart was so damaged by pain and trauma that it could never function the way God intended as long as it stayed wounded. The walls of my heart had crumbled, leaving me exposed, unsafe, and without an inner home. But the fact is, before trauma came to pervert innocence, my heart was a beautiful, pure, original masterpiece created in heaven and sent to earth wrapped in flesh and bone.

The Hebrew and Greek words for "heart" are used almost one thousand times in Scripture, making it the most anthropological term in the Bible. Your heart is such a big deal to God that He writes about it more than anything else—more than sin, more than works, more than obedience, even more than love. And according to God, the heart He designed actually determines the course of your life. Your original heart isn't a bad thing, because it was dreamed up by a good Father who only creates good things.

The Hebrew word for heart is *lebab,* meaning the center of all physical and spiritual life—your core where your feelings, will, and intellect reside. The New Testament Greek word for heart, *kardia,* means thoughts or feelings (mind) and is also defined as the middle. In our modern culture we have often reduced the heart down to a feeling factory. However, though the heart is where your feelings originate, it's far more complex and intricate. Every one of your emotions and thoughts grows like a tree out of your core beliefs, revealing your heart on each matter. Your heart can feel heavy or feel full, or it can turn cold in self-protection. Your heart can be broken, it can ache, or it can be light.

This center inside is the part that makes you special and unique, distinguishing you from the other seven billion people on the planet, even more so than your physical body. Twins might look identical on the outside, but the contents of their hearts make them completely different individuals.

I'm pretty sure I came out of the womb with a microphone, ready for the stage. The moment I discovered how my daddy's video camera captured my performances so I could show them off to people on a screen, I spent hours on the fireplace hearth at our little West Texas home, making up dances and songs to sing into my hairbrush as each moment was recorded. So when my baby brother, Michael, came home from the hospital and Daddy's camera shifted the lens from my performances to this new member of our family, I wasn't exactly overjoyed about sharing the spotlight—especially with someone who just lay there. Shot after shot would begin with Michael cooing on a blanket, until my three-year-old head would slowly begin to creep into the frame, making sure I was still front and center. My dad would video a family barbecue and interview cousins and relatives, and I would run in and practically sit on top of them to monopolize the conversation.

For many years, this documentation of my childish behavior was more than embarrassing. Although I would laugh along with the family as they reminisced about my annoying tendencies, deep inside I was mortified about how consumed I'd been with being seen and heard as a little kid.

Until one day, as an adult, my heavenly Father spoke to my spirit.

"Christa, there's nothing to be ashamed of, since I am the One who created your heart that way. You were simply acting out what I had placed inside of you—living out your original heart design. Beautiful one, can't you see? I created you to be seen and heard for My glory, and you knew that from birth and just acted accordingly."

This newfound revelation of the heart that God gave me flipped my condemning perceptions on their head, and I could begin to see this part of my life as He did—as a gift that simply needed to be unwrapped through maturity, time, and sanctification. My original heart, designed by God, was my dearest friend, hosting the magnificent contents of a one-of-a-kind *me*.

The original design of your heart was never intended to be changed—because the design of your heart is *good*.

God rolled up His sleeves one day long ago, masterfully fashioning your heart as the center of your universe—the mainframe computer, command center, and home base. He picked up certain ingredients like a chef in a kitchen, adding a little bit of this personality trait, a pinch of that talent and gifting. And when your body was done baking in your mother's womb and popped out of the oven, your heart became the place where you made all your decisions that turned into actions. The heart is the eyes and ears that can taste, see, and experience God, producing deep understanding and spiritual discernment. God fashioned your heart with a bent towards certain wants and needs that make you an individual, displaying the nature of your colorful personality.

When my son Moses was just a baby, I would lay him on his tummy and put several brightly colored toys in front of him to play with. But he would usually ignore the big things to focus on a tiny speck of dirt on our floor or the stitches on his blanket. As he grew older and started to walk, Moses wasn't really interested in climbing on top of coffee tables or scaling bookshelves. His father, on the other hand, was apparently a little monkey when he was little—ignoring details to find his way to the top of everything, wanting to look out and see the big picture. My mother-in-law tells stories of Luke as a tiny toddler climbing kitchen cabinets, breaking out of his crib, even ending up on the roof before his second birthday.

We didn't teach Moses to be detail oriented, just as my husband wasn't taught to want to climb on top of everything—which points to the original, uniquely created design of the heart. Yet, the same way I delight in watching my extroverted little boy walking around an entire room full of strangers, desiring to form connection through chatting and physical touch, God delights in watching your heart bloom with specific desires that He placed within you, reflecting different facets of His nature.

Some of you live in search of another carefree adventure, and others want things to line up safely before you leap off a cliff. Some need the strength that comes from solitude, and others desire the energy produced from a room full of strangers. I happened to pop out at birth created to desire music, a stage, and the beauty of words, but my brother, Michael, came out skilled with numbers, problem solving, and a knack for coding and building robots. If my mother had enrolled him in musical theater and sent me to engineering camp, she would have had some cranky kids moping around the house, neither one of us thriving outside of our unique design.

The created heart is never your enemy, but instead is like a building that holds the contents of the real you formed at conception—your authentic and individual self. Your heart comes alive when you are doing what you were created to do, making it silly for you to try to be someone you are not. "We have become His poetry," the apostle Paul tells the Ephesians, "a recreated people that will fulfill the destiny He has given each of us, for we are joined to Jesus, the Anointed One. Even before we were born, God planned in advance our destiny and the good works we would do to fulfill it" (Ephesians 2:10 TPT). As the designing architect of your life, God crafted the framework of your heart, providing everything you need to fulfill and carry out your God-given destiny.

THE REDEEMED HEART

As a wife, mom, and full-time author and speaker, I don't get much time to myself these days. But each morning that I walk my son to school, or lay my head down to go to sleep, or steal away to the loo, I usually stop and take a few deep breaths, checking in with my heart. I have found that one of the most important things I can do is connect deeply with my inner world to see how I'm doing.

"Heart, how are you today, my friend?"

At times, my heart responds by telling me that it's overwhelmed with all that's on my plate. If it's honest, it might be frustrated with a situation or hurting because of the cruel words of a friend. Many times it's overflowing with awe and gratitude, joy and peace, but sometimes it's angry, impatient, or fearful. As I check in with my heart the way I'm checking in on a best friend, I've learned to extend kindness, patience, and understanding.

Especially when my heart is broken.

God's ultimate plan for you isn't simply to hold your hand while you survive the punches of life. He never intended your heart to fragment, tatter, and remain broken to pieces by a broken world. He wants you to be so aware of your heart that you hand it over to Him to clean it up, mature it, and make it whole while you walk with Him.

Your heart was not perfected at salvation, even though all of us would have liked for it to be. Salvation provides us with a banqueting table full of everything we will ever need to thrive, but it's our decision whether or not to sit down, pick up the golden fork, and begin to feast on the abundance of our heavenly inheritance.

When your body dies and your spirit leaves this earth, you might be certain of an eternity with God because of salvation, but as long as your heart remains broken with pain and trauma—hosting the lies of shame, bitterness, inadequacy, and fear deep inside—salvation cannot complete its work through sanctification.

Beautiful friend, Jesus died to give you abundance. His gift of grace is the most powerful gift we will ever have in our possession. Grace keeps us in right standing before God, even as we fail miserably while learning how to walk into newness of life. Grace empowers us to let Father evict our pain monsters, all while He wipes our tears and kisses our wounds. Grace acknowledges that maturity is a relational process and not a destination called perfection. Grace fills our hearts with the resurrection power of Jesus, bringing dead things to life. Grace makes wholeness a possibility for us while we live as mortals, ensuring that *nothing on this earth can ever separate our hearts from the power, presence, and love of God* (see Romans 8:38–39).

When all of the parts of your being—your spirit, heart, soul, mind, and body—are allowed to be purified by the Spirit alive within, each part begins to work together as one, and you finally experience the most authentic expression of yourself on planet earth. When your heart is made whole, your truest identity joins together with the spiritual reality of who God created you to be.

Your heart is secure when it's defined by peace.

Your heart doesn't feel lost because it's been forever found.

Your heart can't be lonely when you have never been abandoned.

And your heart isn't fearful when love overflows inside.

If you want your life to transform, then you must first allow your heart to transform. In order to do that, you must do what you might have avoided. You must start paying close attention to your heart through the lens of the Holy Spirit. The building of your heart was never intended to be ignored and forgotten while life continues to smash it up. It was created to flourish in surrender, to be cleansed with salvation, healed by heaven, rebuilt with grace, and occupied by Love. Your heart was intended to be the safe house where you coexist in relationship with the Trinity who lives inside. When this dance of unity between your original self and God happens, pure life can't help but pour out of the secret place.

Friend, no matter how long your heart has hosted deep pain, endured the monsters that feasted on your soul, and felt shattered by the wrecking balls of trauma, I have amazing news for you: The most powerful person in the universe is already waiting inside, and if you let Him, He will restore everything that pain has stolen from your life, binding up your broken heart and teaching you to walk in freedom.

Open-Heart Surgery

1. If trauma is anyplace in your heart where your pain stays greater than your joy, then is there any place in your heart that fits that definition? What are traumas that might still be lodged in your heart, affecting your life and keeping you from joy?

2. If Trauma A is the *absence* of everything you should have received, but didn't, then has your heart been punched by this kind of pain? Write out any Trauma A you have experienced. Trauma B includes all the things that shouldn't have happened to you, but did. Write out any Trauma B experiences that wounded your heart over the years.

3. If your heart is carrying around old pain, that pain will get extremely heavy, causing you to figure out ways and means to cope. Do you have any unhealed pain that you stuffed down in order to keep functioning? If the answer is yes, write about any escape hatches or coping mechanisms to protect yourself from that pain.

4. For most of my life, I saw my heart as a great enemy, not a friend that God created to house the contents of *me*. Take several moments and think about the original design of your heart. What were you like as an infant or kid? Think about God's design of your heart—what you like/dislike, your personality traits, and your dreams growing up. Have you seen this heart as an enemy, or as a friend? If you're honest, have you loved this heart well, or hated it for being wounded? Write your thoughts about your heart.

5. Take a few moments, close your eyes and fill your lungs, and check in with your heart. Ask, *"Heart, how are you today, my friend?"* What is your heart saying to you today? What is it really feeling? What condition is it in—is it thriving or surviving? Write your answers without using a condemning filter to shame yourself.

Chapter 3

The Doubting Heart

O n May 26, 1988, my husband, Lucas (or Studhub, as I like to fondly refer to him), decided to spend the evening of his sixth birthday doing what little boys do best—getting dirty while exploring the wooded creek next to his house. The air dripped with usual Louisiana humidity from a sticky-hot summer as Luke kicked rocks into shallow water, looking for a crawdad to catch, a vine to swing on, or a frog to torment.

As he jumped along, swatting mosquitos with a stick and trampling the tall grass, his little foot made a discovery that his eyes only wished they had made first. Stomping down onto an old ladder concealed by an overgrowth of green, little Luke let out a scream.

Pain. Searing pain shot through his body, originating from the sole of his left foot.

Looking down, he saw something small poking through his worn yellow Converse, pinning rubber and flesh to rotting wood. The long, rusty nail had done exactly what nails do best—penetrated everything.

What if Luke had decided just to ignore the pain when it began throbbing that day? What if he reasoned that the pain wasn't important enough to warrant looking down?

Ignoring pain would mean:

(a) He might have to live attached to a ladder by the creek, which would be quite limiting.

(b) His wound would never be able to fully heal as long as the nail was still inside, probably getting infected and causing him to limp through life.

(c) The real problem would never be fixed.

Many of us have taught ourselves to treat our heart pain this way. But when we choose to ignore the screaming signals within our inner realm, we might not die, but we end up crippled, unable to run the race we're created to run. Denial about pain keeps our focus off the main issues and original wounds, making it impossible ever to heal and move on completely.

You see, the problem that day in the woods wasn't little Luke's pain—*the problem was the nail.* The pain actually helped him discover his stab wound—the same way emotional pain helps you uncover the stabs that have thrashed at your heart over the years. Pain's main function is to alert your focus to the real problem, or wound, betrayal, or hurt. Without the much-needed aid of pain working in our lives, an ignored gunshot hole might bleed out and cause death, a body could go undiagnosed with internal cancer, and an emotional heart might stay broken, handicapping you through life.

Acknowledgment of your current pain is the most powerful first step towards healing. Instead of running from your wounds, as you might have done in the past, it's time to turn around and face them, realizing that pain itself is not the problem. But when that pain remains unhealed, filling the real estate of your heart with monsters like shame, fear, anger, and bitterness, it's overstayed its welcome. If the pain designed to help you becomes the kind of pain that harms you, it's time to confront it head on.

UNHEALED PAIN

When I began combing through and mapping out patterns from my past with one of my pastors, through the lens of the Holy Spirit, I noticed that friend after friend kept loving me and then leaving me. I would eventually find new friends, but with gaping wounds in my heart that never knew how to heal, my new crew would find themselves at the mercy of my old, wounded behaviors. At some point (usually around the two-year mark), people began pulling away as if I had been dipped in poisonous repellent.

Year after year, as the same abandonment scenario kept playing out with different characters, I had to face the difficult reality that the only common denominator in the equation was *me*. Over the years, as an adult scared of opening my smashed-up heart to any more wounding humans, my extroverted personality had gradually withdrawn and I had become a recluse, trying my best to avoid deep friendships that required more than a text or Instagram comment. I had no idea how to be myself anymore, whoever she was, and I was never truly authentic, since that girl seemed to eventually be cast aside. To cope with the agony of a lifetime of rejection, I learned either to have "best friends" who lived across the country, or to keep locals at a safe distance.

If you watched my life on social media sites, the year prior to Goldie's birth looked like a California dream. But in reality, each day felt more like a nightmare. Repeated difficulties were exposing unresolved anger issues, old hurts, relational disasters—and before I knew it, disappointment and betrayal had piled up into a mountain that I just couldn't climb on my own. The longer I tried to fix myself, without success, the more my heart shut down on me, unable to keep functioning under the weight of hurts that had piled high. As the brokenness got heavier, filling my heart with contents that I didn't understand, wounds kept ruining everything, including my marriage and closest relationships.

During my first two years of marriage, Luke and I tended to swing between the newlywed high and the reality of two broken people who kept rubbing up against each other like sandpaper. Although we had put a covenant around our relationship, pledging to live in close proximity to each other's pain for better or for worse, it was getting harder and harder to stay close while our self-protective claws kept emerging to rip each other to shreds. We didn't attract what we wanted—we attracted who we were—and we were both wounded in different ways. My husband had promised to love a girl who believed she was unlovable, which unfortunately meant he encountered an angry fighter who pushed away the very love he was giving, believing she didn't deserve it. Sadly, that love had produced an anger deep inside me that kept punching at a boy already burdened with feelings of inadequacy, beating him down even lower instead of building him up.

Over the years, we had figured out how to bury a few hatchets to keep life rolling along, but eventually those open wounds from the first years of marriage—the wounds we had tried unsuccessfully to hide and ignore with time and denial—had finally festered into a pattern of constant fighting and offense.

One day, as the warm sun streamed into our apartment in Los Angeles, I lay on the floor of our living room, shaking an imaginary fist full of accusations at the sky, exhausted from a recent screaming match that ended with Luke storming away and driving off to who knows where.

"God, You were so clear in the beginning, giving us both the green light to get married! So why did You lead us both into a relationship that continues to destroy us both with pain?"

I can't begin to tell you the number of times I have found myself in this scenario, hurling anger at heaven, questioning the goodness of God after life and love had mauled my heart. I also can't count the times I've heard others screaming out to God demanding the same answers, making this a very valid question that we have permission to ask.

"God, if You're really good, then why do bad things keep happening?"

As a good Christian girl who felt guilty about everything, my mouth knew all the religious answers to chant in unison during a church service, such as, *"God is good—all the time—all the time, God is good!"* I would spout Scripture about how He had a plan to prosper me and not to harm me

(Jeremiah 29:11), assuring others that He would somehow work out my mess for good (Romans 8:28). But deep down in the honesty zone, I didn't really believe that to be true.

Almost every time I would go through a trial, I would immediately put God on trial. Someone would get sick, and though we would pray and believe in accordance with Scripture, the person would die, and a piece of my heart would grow cold and bitter with blame. I would feel led to change jobs, but then the whole experience would explode in my face, and I would pull away from God in wounded disappointment. I would pray and cry out to the Almighty for a breakthrough in a certain area, but when freedom wouldn't come quickly, I'd throw up my hands, convinced that He liked to ignore me more than help me.

How could my heart believe the truth when parts of it felt abandoned by a seemingly distant God whom I didn't know how to hear and that I couldn't experience? Though I was faithful to read His words in my Bible, pray towards a faraway heaven, and send worship songs up to an invisible blob in the sky, I didn't have a clue how to turn my dutiful Christianity into a two-way relationship on earth where God was present, and very real. No matter how hard I tried, I could never get close to Someone who, deep down, I was pushing away in distrust.

"ARE YOU SURE GOD IS GOOD?"

Our hearts can either be guarded *from* God in doubt and distrust, or peace will guard our hearts through relationship as we abide *in* Christ.

When the serpent slithered into the garden of Eden, whispering poisonous lies into the ears, minds, and hearts of a sinless Adam and Eve, Satan had one primary goal in mind: to make sure that God's children began to question the goodness of their perfect Father. I can only imagine him hissing deception into their pure innocence.

"Are you sure you can trust God? See, He doesn't want you to eat the fruit because you will be like Him. This world He's set up for you and the parameters He gave you, they're not in your best interest. You need to take matters into your own hands to protect yourself. Eat of the fruit and you will be like Him—knowing good from evil. Believe me, guys, He cannot be trusted. *God is not a good Father.*"

As Adam and Eve let into their minds the possibility that God didn't love them completely, that He was withholding His best, that His intentions weren't good, and that His word couldn't be trusted, their hearts were opened up to deadly deception. As a result, they made a decision to eat the fruit, releasing sin and death upon the world—the same fallen world that continues to smash our hearts with pain today.

The deceiver knows that if he can get you to question God as a good Father—believing that He doesn't love you fiercely, that He doesn't fight to protect you, that He didn't send His only Son to restore you to His embrace—then you will begin to withhold pieces of your heart from Him, just as I did.

Our scheming enemy also knows that as long as parts of your heart aren't on friendly terms with God, even though you might be born again, those places will remain barren, tormented, fragmented, and broken—the way mine was for decades, even as a dedicated follower of Jesus. I had been like Adam and Eve in the garden, letting the serpent hiss into my ear and convince the broken parts of my heart that God wasn't good. I built a secret case against Him over years of pain, and as the case file grew bigger, filled with truthful facts of personal trauma and tragedy in a fallen world, my heart divided into the healed parts that truly loved Him and the wounded parts that were more than skeptical.

Although you can never be separated from the love of God, you can definitely live like you are. And because perception can determine your spiritual reality, if your heart is shielding itself from God and His love, then you're going to have a hard time experiencing and hearing the very One you're trying to push away. You will put up walls inside, consciously or subconsciously, refusing to let Him get too close. You will section off broken parts plagued with fear, afraid to let Him draw near. You will hide struggles in shame, petrified of letting Him see. As long as your heart isn't sure that He's good, you will never fully experience the peace that passes understanding that guards your heart and mind in Christ Jesus (Philippians 4:7).

When my life finally hit a rock-bottom-hopeless zone, I needed a Savior who was more powerful than the hurt ruining my life. The burden of my offense towards God, myself, and others had grown too heavy to carry around anymore, and I was finally willing to surrender, to ask the Holy Spirit to help me see that God was good in the midst of all the bad.

THE DIAMOND CAVE

When you lie down at God's feet in surrender to tell Him that you are willing to do anything to get your heart healed, you had better be prepared for some unexpected twists in your story. Mine came when Luke and I felt God pulling us from sunny Los Angeles to the last place on earth we ever expected—back to little Abilene, Texas, where I grew up and couldn't leave fast enough as a teenager. My due date to meet Luca Gold was just two months away, and I was desperate to get some painful loose ends tied up in my life before I had the opportunity to pass those devastating issues on to my daughter.

One chilly January afternoon, after settling into a furnished rental around the corner from my parents' house, I wrapped the sides of my cardigan tightly around a belly filled with life and sunk deeply into a big floral chair across from my therapist mother, ready for some inner healing ministry. Closing my eyes and sighing deeply, I knew that my soul needed answers that I hadn't been able to find on my own; my mom was committed to praying with me as we asked Jesus to bring all the broken parts of my heart back together.

With a head bowed in reverent prayer and eyes closed tightly, I began to approach the throne of Father with the boldness and confidence of a hurting, but determined woman. I didn't need more head knowledge or memorized Scriptures. I didn't need another sermon or self-help book. My heart needed an *encounter* with Someone more real and powerful than the pain that kept eating me alive.

"Father," I whispered softly, "search me and know me. I don't have a clue what's going on inside—everything feels so confusing. All I know is that my wounds are destroying my life and the lives of those I love. Please, Abba, will You help me understand what is really going on deep down and heal this pain?"

As if a curtain was lifted on a movie screen, a scene began to play out within, and the eyes of my heart opened to the most beautiful sight I had ever seen.

I was standing directly in front of Jesus.

Deep pools of the purest affection sparkled in His green eyes, reflecting an ocean of love as endless as the heavens. Like an inescapable pull of gravity towards the earth, His gaze seemed to pull my heart straight from my chest, singing an unsung melody that drew every cell of my being into a safe harbor of pure love.

My physical body might have been sinking into an ordinary chair, but with eyes closed and a posture of surrendered prayer, my heart was being led into an encounter with a beautifully real God—more real than anything I had seen living with eyes wide open. Jesus was a tangible person as accessible as the air. And He wanted to spend time with me more than anything in the world.

The longer I stared into His face filled with compassion, the more my weary soul began to let down the walls I had built in protection around my wounds. As I gazed directly into strength greater than all my problems, the violent winds of worry began to calm within. The affection of this man was so sure, His arms were strong and inviting, and there was something about His smile that assured me that joy was always available in this place.

Then everything changed. Suddenly a dense wall of dark smoke began to rise out of the ground in front of my feet, stretching far into the sky—separating me from Jesus. As I watched the blackness fill the air, panic began to claw like a monster inside, choking out the peace I had just found. The harder I looked for Him, the less I could see anything at all. The more desperate I was to get back to His gaze, the faster hope drained from my soul.

"Jesus!" my heart prayed frantically in the blackness. "What is this wall between us, and how do I get back to You?"

Silence. I watched myself running up and down the wall, feeling for an opening but finding none. Something began to twist in my gut, my panic giving way to something far more sinister.

Deepest rage.

The heart that just minutes before had been overwhelmed with affection and devotion to the God I had pledged my life to now began hardening into stone. The reality was, a part of me was furious at the man standing on the other side of the wall. With fists clenched, jaw tight, and face reddened with rage, I threw back my head and did what I had wanted to do for many years. I started shouting at Him.

"Why do You keep letting me down with broken promises that seem more like suggestions, Jesus? Aren't You supposed to be powerful? Aren't You supposed to love me, God? What a joke!"

With years of training myself in obedient composure, it felt frightening to let the hot lava spill from my lips. But this volcano was erupting.

"Why do You keep allowing me to be rejected, betrayed, and abandoned by people who claim to love me? You promised me freedom in all areas, so when are You going to deliver on Your word? I can't do this anymore! So many of my relationships are broken, and so are Your promises! In fact, keep Your promises to Yourself, Jesus, because I can't handle being disappointed by them anymore when they don't materialize. How am I supposed to believe You when You don't do what You say?"

My heart raced as I felt myself pacing back and forth in the vision. Shaking my fists at a darkened sky, I screamed out again, "I should be further along than I am at this point in my life, and I've done everything I know to do. So how do You expect me to become all You want when You keep allowing this world to crush me?"

Like a devouring monster liberated from a lifetime of captivity, I threw my head back one last time to release my heart's deepest, guttural scream.

"I'm angry at You, Jesus! I don't trust You! And I hate You for not protecting me!"

Crumpling helplessly into a pile of sobs on the floor of my naked heart, my physical body sat weeping, heavy with the weight of an ugly reality. I had asked to see my whole heart, and God had eagerly answered my prayer—but I wasn't prepared for what I saw. With eyes closed tight, tears pouring off my chin, I was painfully conscious of the broken heart inside that brewed with toxic bitterness towards the God I longed to love. This was the real me—all of me— finally exposed by the light of the truth. I wasn't able to love God with my whole heart because this part of my heart, offended by wounds and angry from pain, felt that He was the one who had let it shatter into a million pieces.

That afternoon I realized that at its core, the offended, broken pieces of my heart didn't believe that God was good. How could He be, when so many bad things continued to happen, causing so much pain? My wounded heart had built a solid case against the goodness of God through a lifetime of bad experiences, and it wasn't going to be convinced otherwise by listening to another sermon telling me facts about God's faithfulness. I needed to *believe*—and that required a supernatural encounter with a love greater than my brokenness.

"Christa!"

I looked up suddenly, peering with curiosity into the blackness, alarmed by the firm, confident, but kind voice of Jesus as it thundered through the wall and shook my core.

"I knew the fall of man was going to happen, and that life and people would break your fragile heart. So I gave you the ability to guard yourself, even urging you in Proverbs 4:23 to 'guard your heart above all else, for it determines the course of your life.'"

He paused for a moment and let out a deep, painful sigh.

"But beautiful girl, *I never intended you to guard your heart from Me.*"

Like a husband forced to listen to the distant sobs of his wife as she lay beaten and bruised by an intruder, Jesus had endured years of my painful wails without being invited in close to help bandage the wounds. While on the outside I looked all together and had said yes to Him at an early age, over time I had kicked Him out onto the streets, accusing and condemning Him for all the bad things that had happened over the years. But instead of turning to walk away, Jesus had waited faithfully at the door of my heart, knocking—simply believing, crying, praying, strategizing, and moving heaven and earth to be reunited with the one He loved enough to die for—the wounded, confused, and bitter me. After years of being rejected, this man didn't just want me if I was fixed and perfect, but as I was—broken and bleeding.

What lonely heart doesn't long for a devoted lover? What soul doesn't burn to be the object of someone's undying affection? After decades of my cold bitterness, this Love had never wavered, never given up hope, and never stopped believing in me, even when parts of me had stopped believing in Him. He had fought for my heart against many foes with violent fury, but always with the gentle tenderness of a lover. He had chosen me before I had chosen Him, having me on His mind when He was gushing with blood and nailed to a cross. My Jesus had always wanted me, always loved me, always longed for me—everything my heart had ever dreamed of.

Here I was, finally realizing that the one thing I had been searching for was wrapped up in the One who was always available—the Jesus who had never left me and never forsaken me. God hadn't abandoned me as a little girl, as I had once believed; I had abandoned the hope of His goodness when pain had become too heavy to bear on my own. God hadn't left me to be tormented by a cruel world; He was heartbroken that I had been broken by the fall of man. And He was longing to come in to heal and restore all that had been lost.

As if an old, dirty veil had been lifted from my eyes, I saw myself standing to my feet. My mind raced, bursting with hopeful anticipation for the first time in years.

"Jesus, I'm so sorry!" I called out loudly through the blackness, tears of godly sorrow pouring out like blood from a wound, leading my heart into true repentance through the patient persistence of a kind Savior. "I'm so sorry I've been offended, dividing my heart and keeping parts of it from You. I can't do this anymore—I can't live without You in every area of my life. Please, Jesus! How do I get to You?"

With the simple logic a little child could understand, I heard Jesus chuckling.

"Well, Christa," He responded. "You simply have to ask."

Before my mind could even formulate a thought, I was screaming in desperation at the top of my lungs, "Jesus, please—I want You! I want You! I need You!"

Just like that, my spinning world screeched to a peaceful halt. The ominous darkness began to twist and swirl, pushed aside by a glowing figure lit with such brilliance that I shielded my eyes into a squint, but I didn't dare look away. The man splitting the darkness wasn't weak and feeble, speaking in hushed tones and silent whispers. This man was a warring conqueror, magnificent and mighty, bursting with unmatched strength that sliced effortlessly through the darkness that held me captive. This man had never had a true adversary, for nothing could ever defeat Him, and His eyes burned with such fierce passion that my body went weak at the knees.

As I lowered my defenses and gave Jesus full access to every part of my broken heart, finally letting go of the distrust that had poisoned my soul, the black wall in front of me didn't disappear as I expected. Instead, it began to transform in front of my eyes, morphing into a beautiful wall of brilliant black diamonds that stretched out into the sky. I looked up in awe at a sight too heavenly to comprehend with an earthly mind, but Jesus wasn't finished with His extravagant display of power. Confidently He reached back to put His hand onto the breathtaking black diamonds, and as His fingertips touched the perfect jewels, the most brilliant light began to radiate from His hand. Huge white diamonds grew outward and climbed upward over the wall, covering the dark jewels with the brilliance of heaven's whitest light. I could only stare at this massive wall that shined, sparkled, and radiated with the glow of pure glory. Jesus stood in His strength, never taking His eyes off of my face, locked in with a love that would never let go.

Just as I thought my heart couldn't take any more, the entire wall began to bend slowly, stretching out over my head to curve into a perfect dome of diamonds surrounding us both. With a thunderous bang, the solid diamond cave sealed into oneness with the ground, and a white bed with fluffy pillows appeared in the center of the room, lowering into the floor.

I turned back to face my Rescuer, whose conquering face had softened into a grin.

"Christa," He said excitedly, eyes reflecting the brilliant diamonds that surrounded us both, "this is what it means to guard your heart, beautiful one. I'm going to teach you how to guard your intimacy with *Me*."

Because I asked Jesus for help, cracking my heart into confessed surrender, He most definitely delivered, teaching me first about a concept I had never understood as a Christian: how to reconcile great tragedy with the goodness of God.

Open-Heart Surgery

1. If pain isn't your enemy, but unhealed pain can become your greatest foe, then can you recognize any wounds in your heart that have become infected over time, poisoning you on the inside? Do these wounds keep recurring, as mine did? Write about any painful patterns you can trace in your life over the years. Are there themes of fear, betrayal, abandonment, abuse, or trauma?

2. When life is hard, have you questioned the goodness of God, as I did? Do you *feel* separated from His love, even though you know He's always there? Take a few moments and close your eyes, being completely honest with yourself. Are you disappointed in God, or feel as though He's forgotten about you? Are there any places in your heart that aren't on friendly terms with Him, even though you love Him? Write out your answers, beginning a truthful, heartfelt conversation.

3. God wants to give you your own secret place where the two of you meet—tailor-made just for you. But before that can happen, you have to be honest about any distrust, bitterness, or anger that you have towards Him that blocks the intimacy between you. Go somewhere quiet, silencing your heart before God. Ask Him, as David did in Psalm 139:23, "Search me, God, and know my heart." Ask to see a picture of the *real* you—not the person you try to be or the person you think you should be. Pour out the real, raw truth about what's in your heart.

The Reconciled Heart

I pulled out my computer and set it on my lap, ready to type at warp speed. I had been invited to be a speaker for a worship school at Bethel Church in Redding, California, and I had time to duck into a session taught by my favorite pastor and hero mentor, Bill Johnson. I knew from past experiences with Bill that using pen and paper wouldn't be a fast-enough way to record all the nuggets of gold wisdom that flew out as he spoke.

As Bill began to talk about the goodness of God and why we worship, my fingers typing at lightning speed, he casually said a sentence that hit me upside the head with earth-rocking, healing revelation: "God is in charge, but God is not in control. If you have kids, you know this to be true. It's God's will that none would perish. Do people perish? Yes. Is it God's will? Absolutely not."

God has a will, and because you're made in His image, you have a will. And though at times your will might rise up with rebellion, anger, judgment, malice, and all sorts of nasty intentions, God's will is always good, pleasing, and perfect.

According to Scripture, the will of a good Father is that *all* of His children—no matter how vile, destructive, perverse, or sinful—would run into His open arms of love through repentance, finding salvation. The apostle Paul wrote, "The Lord is not slack concerning his promise, as some count slackness; but is longsuffering to you-ward, *not wishing that any should perish*, but that all should come to repentance" (2 Peter 3:9 ASV, italics mine). So if it's God's will for every one of His children to be saved and reconciled to His heart while living on this earth, then why doesn't it happen if He's so strong and mighty?

I grew up in church learning big concepts about God—like the fact that He was all-powerful and sovereign. So for many years I misunderstood these descriptions to mean that He was a control freak who orchestrated all the horrible things happening around the world, actually wanting them to happen. Within this theology, no matter what went down, my heart truly believed that God willed it into existence.

When someone died, no matter how horrifically they died, it was all the will of God because it happened—and because lost people probably needed to get saved at the funeral. If a wreck occurred, then God allowed it because it was part of His will and plan. If a hurricane destroyed a city, then God was the judgment mastermind who willed the destruction. If a relationship didn't work out, if someone was abused or orphaned, if someone was born with a handicap, if a cruel dictator was elected, or if I couldn't get free in a certain area, then God must be willing the bad so that He could bring something good out of it later and get the glory.

A man came up to me after I finished speaking at a church on the goodness of God, letting me know that a lot of horrible things had happened to him over the years; but then he shrugged and ended with one of my least favorite statements: "But it's okay, because everything happens for a reason!"

The problem with this "Que Sera, Sera" mindset towards God's will, in which all the hell that happens is made to happen for a greater purpose, is that it inadvertently proposes that God is a baby killer, a cancer giver, a sexual abuser, and a terrorist, discounting a few important factors that shape outcomes every day. And those factors are:

1. Our free will.
2. The free will of others.
3. The fallen world in which we live.
4. A very real enemy who wants to steal from us, kill us, and destroy us.

OUR FREE WILL

When God began fashioning Adam from the dust, then drawing Eve from his side, the Creator made His children in the image of Himself—in the image of Love. And for love to be love, it must always be given a choice.

You see, when the Trinity decided to have kids, if they had crawled inside of our little hearts and programmed us like computers to always love them, we wouldn't be children;

we would be robots. As my dear friend William Paul Young, author of the novel *The Shack*,* so eloquently puts it, "Love forced is not love at all."

When your heart explodes with love for someone, it chooses to give the gift of affection, which is why God gave you a control center deep within your heart that possesses the ability to either choose to love Him or choose to reject Him. Since He created the human heart, giving it the great gift called *free will*, He gave all of us full jurisdiction over our inner realm, including the ability to say "no" to His love, His will, and His ways.

Let that sink in for a second. You are the only one who will ever be in full control of your own heart—not God. He will never violate the control He gave you. You are the supreme ruler of your heart, making the final decisions on what laws are put in place to govern your inner country. And as the sovereign of your life, you can choose to make up your own laws and follow them, or you can submit yourself to God and His ways. Our good God will always be present and willing to be your Counselor, Helper, Protector, Redeemer, Savior, and the Restorer, but you hold the final say. God offers you unconditional love and eternal relationship, but then gives you the freedom to refuse His gift, allowing you to love Him conditionally and refuse the relationship (and fellowship) He's offering.

Right now, my three-year-old son Moses is obsessed with everything "Mama" and literally doesn't want to have any-thing to do with his papa. He wants Mommy to put him in

---

*William Paul Young, *The Shack* (Newbury Park, CA: Windblown Media, 2007).

his car seat, and Mommy to take him out. He wants Mommy to cuddle him in the morning—on the other side of the bed from his dad. As Luke and I chatted about it the other night, he was literally on the verge of tears talking about how painful it is that his son constantly rejects his affection—and there is nothing he can do about it. Luke takes Moses to the park, rides bikes to get ice cream, and plays with him for hours to develop attachment and relationship—being more engaged as a father than I've ever seen in an earthly man. But even with endless amounts of love that Luke sends towards his son, Moses is the only one who can choose to love his father back. And for now, Moses simply doesn't want to be with him.

Love cannot be forced. Love is always a choice. For God to snap His fingers and override your switch called *free will*, invading your heart beyond your control and forcing you to do something you don't choose, would violate His nature and the laws of love. And because God never acts outside of His nature, love never violates. Instead, love always submits.

When I think about this all-powerful, sovereign God submitting and limiting His power to little ol' me and my choices, I go weak at the knees in reverent awe. Did you catch that? Every day, your Almighty Creator chooses to submit Himself to you—His creation.

Over the course of my life, I have watched God yield Himself to the truckloads of bad decisions I've made. My free will chose to steal clothes in high school, resulting in disciplinary consequences enforced by humans, not by the hand of God. My free will chose many times to consume too many recreational substances, resulting in nights hunched over a toilet—and not because God wanted to punish me. My free will chose to speed 90 miles an hour in the pouring rain to catch a flight, hydroplaning my car into a guardrail—and not because God wanted me to learn joy within trials. My free will chose to get wasted one night in high school, resulting in a drunken guy climbing on top of me to do the unthinkable—and not because God had plans to give me a ministry to the sexually assaulted. My free will chose to take punches at my husband in anger, wounding his heart deeply and causing him to pull away in protection—and not because God was a narcissist who couldn't wait to get the glory when He healed our marriage.

When my choices turned my life into a disaster zone, I was the one making the decision to kick God and His ways to the curb. He was always the faithful One interceding on my behalf, waiting with open arms, ready to pick up the pieces, dry my tears, heal my wounds, and save me time and time again.

When we choose badly, then bad things tend to happen. Sometimes it really is as simple as that.

For many months I have warned Moses that chewing his fingernails down to the quick not only is a nasty habit, but can be very painful. Then when his nail chewing resulted in an ingrown, infected fingernail, he burst into tears, getting angry at *me* when I tried to apply the doctor's prescribed ointment.

Many times when we make the wrong decision and all hell breaks loose, the last place we want to look is at ourselves. I didn't want to look at all the bad choices I had made over the years that derailed my life; God was the first person

I blamed every time I collided with disaster. I didn't want to look at all the horrible things I had done to my husband to contribute to his pulling away and growing cold in our marriage. I just wanted to blame him—and then blame God for leading me into the relationship in the first place. I didn't want to acknowledge all of my controlling and manipulative tendencies that caused friends to eventually bolt in protection. I just wanted to blame God for allowing people to keep rejecting me.

When we choose to pick up a hammer and pound down on our fingers—ignoring God's Word, His will, and the relationship He offers—many of us turn around to then blame Him for letting us get hurt. And though Father made His perfect will as plain as day many times throughout Scripture—giving us a manual for life to keep us safe (not to keep us from having a good time)—we are the ones who turn our backs and choose not to pay attention.

God doesn't tell us to abstain from sex until marriage because He's a killjoy who is out of touch with a modern world. He wants to protect our hearts, knowing that before you're naked with someone physically, it's much safer to be naked emotionally and spiritually, putting a covenant around your relationship when everything (the good and the bad) gets exposed through time and friction. He doesn't command you to forgive your hurtful parent, betrayer, or abuser because He doesn't have compassion for what they have done to you. He knows that unresolved bitterness and unforgiveness poisons *you* on the inside, ruining your chances of peace, freedom, and joy. He doesn't ask you to worship because He's an egomaniac who needs constant approval. He knows that you become like the thing you set your heart on, and He knows that you thrive when you're like Him—fully free, full of life, abounding in love, peace, and joy.

Now, there might be things that your heart is still accusing God for that He had absolutely nothing to do with. He gave you the keys to drive the car of your life, with a road map called the Bible and the counseling Holy Spirit to help you stay on track. But ultimately, you're the one who gets to choose which way the wheel turns. And some of you have veered far off the road, turning the wheel of your life into wall after wall, growing angry and bitter at God for allowing you to crash.

If you ever want your heart to be healed, you must first put down your anger and stop blaming your Savior for the wrecks that happened from your bad decisions. Stop accusing Him for the times you have exercised your free will and ended up getting hurt. As long as you keep refusing His roadside assistance, you're going to stay stranded on the side of the road and feeling abandoned—but it's not His will, and it's not His way.

He's your Rescuer after every accident, even if the crash was your fault. He's the Redeemer of all your mistakes—even the ones rooted in rebellion and sin. And He's the Restorer of all that was lost—the good Savior who is waiting to come in with His overwhelming goodness and save the day, time and time again.

THE FREE WILL OF OTHERS

One of my greatest friends was born into a notorious crime family, and to this day, her relatives still run their city with corruption, deceit, and robbery. Because her father and mother were given free will to have sex resulting in her natural conception, an innocent little baby didn't have much of a choice over the less than ideal circumstances she was born into. By the time she was in grade school, her father had her pickpocketing like Oliver Twist on busy streets, able to crack locks and steal from homes. By the time she graduated from high school, jail had become her second home, with a criminal record longer than her report card.

Late one evening, after local law enforcers unlocked her cell and spilled her onto lonely streets once again, her desperate heart reached the end of a hopeless rope. With feet turning towards the edge of town to run away from the hell of life, she cried out to a sky full of stars for answers. As she walked across an open field, a man named Jesus led her heart into radical, supernatural salvation. It was never the will of a good Father for her to be starved, beaten, abused, and used as a commodity to further the corruption in the family business; it was always His will to restore all that had been lost and lead her back to His heart—the place where she belonged.

Every day, our powerful God named Unconditional Love submits Himself to the bad choices of His children throughout the world—including your parents, leaders, abusers, bullies, and captors. But I guarantee you, God always has endless strategies, plans, prayers, angels, and supernatural power to get every child back into the arms of love—no matter how far they have fallen. Paul tells the Romans, "He knows us far better than we know ourselves, knows our pregnant condition, and keeps us present before God. That's why we can be so sure that every detail in our lives of love for God is worked into something good" (Romans 8:28 MSG).

That is the way and the will of our good, good Father— the Creator of life. He never ceases to breathe into places destroyed by death to make them come alive. That is the fullness of Romans 8:28—not that God is willing all of the bad, but that you had better believe that He uses every bit of it, always working to bring good out of every situation.

Your story might not be as tragic as my friend's childhood nightmare of crime, but it's impossible to avoid the punches of others while living in close proximity to human beings. No matter how sparkling your home life was, I guarantee that you have been blindsided by the choices of family members, friends, and strangers who shattered your heart, your property, and your body. The free will of others crushes our lives out of left field through all sorts of unforeseen circumstances.

Back in college while working as a summer camp counselor, I met a tall, dark, handsome boy with deep blue eyes who quickly stole my heart out of my chest. He was getting ready to enter full-time ministry, traveling the world to love and serve the poor and orphaned—which swept this twenty-year-old Christian girl right off her feet.

Because he lived a state away, we made a few trips to see one another, emailing back and forth and calling when long-distance prices would allow. I would pray with anticipation, excited that God seemed to be leading us together, possibly even bringing me a husband. When I was asked to play violin for his brother's wedding, I responded before blinking, feeling like a little schoolgirl about to burst at the opportunity to see him again. But after spending a good week coming up with cute outfits and imagining clever things to say, I got to the wedding only to be ignored. The same boy who had shown romantic interest turned a cold, heartless shoulder, acting all weekend as if we had never met. After the wedding ended, I crawled into bed and curled up into a fetal position, sobbing and angry that God would tease me with an open door that brutally slammed in my face.

Although you will always be the ruler of your own heart through your choices, you have very little, if anything, to do with the choices of others—just as I had nothing to do with that boy's decision to reject me so cruelly. God loved him enough to let him make that decision. But this is where God takes the most punches—bearing the blame when the free will of others leaves us broken and bleeding.

The free will of others will continue to negatively impact all of our lives, and pain will be the result. But if we choose to draw close to God in our pain—instead of running away in distrust—miracles are always the result.

In 1 Samuel 16, God showed His will for Israel by anointing David as king, but the current king put up a fight. King Saul jealously sought to kill David, chasing him into the wilderness for eleven years and causing him all sorts of trouble. But in the pain as he cried out to God, David's heart was grounded in intimacy, and many of our powerful Psalms were written from the depth of that relationship. Likewise, the apostle Paul was stoned, chased out of cities, arrested repeatedly, and put into prison countless times as a believer. But because He used his persecution to draw deeper into the heart of God, most of our New Testament was written, and salvations, miracles, and signs and wonders poured out of his life.

Remember, Jesus said, "I have told you these things, so that in me you may have peace. In this world *you will have trouble*. But take heart! I have overcome the world" (John 16:33 NIV, italics mine). We are never promised that we can escape the trials and tribulations in our fallen world, as evidenced all throughout Scripture. But if we stay in relationship with the source, we can develop trust. And out of that trust, we can have peace in the midst of every storm.

WE LIVE IN A FALLEN WORLD

In a fallen world, none of us escapes the pain that comes with being human. The first place you encountered trauma was probably within your family. You had zero control over what kind of care you had as a newborn, and your heart learned very quickly whether or not life was going to be safe or very, very scary. Because you came into this world dependent on both the good and bad choices of others, you may have started off life with a smashed-up heart and a list of facts proving how this world is horribly unsafe.

On top of all that, you were born into systems, governments, countries, and religions that were established centuries before you came along. Though we always hope that our leaders will protect us, many decisions around the world are made because of greed, commerce, power, and money—*and not at all because God wanted them to.* Wars are fought, dictators destroy countries, and corruption bleeds into nations because God loves us all enough to let us reject Him. And over the course of history, we sure have made a lot of unfathomable choices that were far from His perfect will. Those bad choices have affected us all.

The more you learn about the toxic chemicals and pesticides that are allowed in and on our foods, water sources, and household products, the more you see that rising cancer rates and chronic illnesses aren't always a strange phenomenon—or an act of God. Of course, not all disease is caused by our environment; people suffer from terrible infirmities of unknown cause. But that doesn't mean disease is God's will any more than it was His will that evil entered the world. He sent Jesus in skin and bones to show us the will of the Father against infirmity as His Son healed the sick, raised the dead, cleansed the leper, and drove out demons (Matthew 10:8). Nevertheless, God often gets the blame when people get sick or die from illness.

The further the curtain is drawn back to reveal the deviant political choices made for power, finance, and selfish gain, the more our economic crashes are proven to be the cause and effect of greed—and not the Father's cruel plan to teach us all a lesson. Jesus came to display the will of His Abba—setting up a new government on earth as it is in heaven (Matthew 6:10). But many times, God still gets the blame when financial hardship affects our world.

The more you learn about nature and what our modern

conveniences are doing to the environment—dumping large amounts of toxic trash into the ocean to kill sea creatures, letting our cars and product production spew out emissions that pollute the air, digging and drilling dangerously under the ground for oil regardless of the long-term consequences, and how all of this affects the weather, earth, and ecosystem—the more you see how mankind might have more to do with a lot of the world's natural disasters than the God who commissioned us to take care of the home He gave us (Psalm 115:16). But many times, God still gets the blame when our poor care of the planet results in calamity.

The longer we find ourselves exposed to the institution of the Western church, unfortunately, the more lies, corruption, deceit, cheating, jealousy, addiction, control, manipulation, and ambition we end up seeing within the hearts of wounded human leaders. I have met Christian after Christian who has been abused and misused by leaders who fail to model the *real* Jesus—but it isn't His will, and it definitely isn't His abusing way. If you have any doubt about Jesus' kind, loving, forgiving, empowering leadership skills, refresh your memory by reading the first four books of the New Testament.

God is not behind every outcome, orchestrating chaos like a malevolent puppeteer. His sovereign nature operates only inside the law of love, and because He *is* love, He loves us all enough to give us choices, even when they destroy us, others, the church, and the planet.

THE REAL ENEMY

The other day, as Moses finished an episode of the biblical cartoon series *Superbook*, he looked up at me with concern. He had watched the battle between Lucifer and the angels of God, watching Satan fall from heaven to earth, then deceiving Adam and Eve in the garden to gain power on the earth through sin and death.

"Mommy," he said, "I don't want to have disobedience in my heart, because that gives power to that bad angel, Lucifer. I want to have obedience in my heart to give power to God and all of His angels! Let's always believe God, okay?"

My mouth dropped open, realizing that my three-year-old son understood and believed in the spiritual realm more than many adult Christians do. From a little cartoon and our teaching in the home, Moses understood that the contents of his heart gave power to an outer, unseen world, and he wanted to believe God so that the good guys would have the power in his life.

Because we live in a natural world that can be seen and felt, at times it takes extra effort to remember Paul's reminder in Ephesians 6:12: "For we are not fighting against flesh-and-blood enemies, but against evil rulers and authorities of the unseen world, against mighty powers in this dark world, and against evil spirits in the heavenly places" (NLT). I don't like to focus on the enemy—I'd rather focus on the God who easily defeated him. But at the same time, it would be very foolish of me to ignore the Devil, pretending that he wasn't prowling around like a roaring lion, seeking to devour, kill, steal, and destroy me and my family (John 10:10; 1 Peter 5:8).

This deceiver is the ruler of our fallen world that's filled with sin, sickness, and death. And as long as our hearts agree with his lies, then he will have power and authority.

But at the end of the day, Satan is not the enemy of God—He is a created being whom God has the power to squash like a bug. When *we* chose disobedience in the garden of Eden and empowered *our* enemy, the Author of Life had already planned out His rescue mission to save us. God's will has always been to hide us safely in Christ, making us new creations, and giving us the authority to live on this earth as it is in heaven.

Child of God, your Father is always good to you, and the Devil is always bad. And though the enemy still has power on the earth through our agreement, our good Father will always bring life out of everything that the Devil comes to destroy.

RECONCILED

If our hearts are not anchored to the goodness of God when tragedy strikes, we lower our theology to match our pain. We forget who the good guy is, and who the bad guy is. We forget that "The reason the Son of God appeared was to destroy the works of the devil" (1 John 3:8 ESV). And the works of the Devil include horrible things like stealing, killing, and destroying. We forget that "God is light; in him there is no darkness at all" (1 John 1:5 NIV), and that Jesus came so that we could have life, and have it abundantly (John 10:10). We forget that God didn't orchestrate the fall of man, resulting in our fallen human condition. We forget that the enemy is the ruler of this world, bringing sickness and death—like the anencephaly that killed my daughter.

When indescribable tragedy crashes into our hearts, it's easy to forget that we are children of the King. But when the unimaginable happened to me, my Jesus came on a special black ops rescue mission to take back all authority in heaven and on earth and place the keys of the kingdom into my hands.

I am a believer, and I have been given the same authority that Jesus had over sickness and death. I am a Christian, and the same resurrection power that raised Christ from the dead now lives inside of me. I know how to pray the will of God according to Matthew 6:10, asking His kingdom to come "on earth as it is in heaven." Because there are no wars in heaven, I pray peace to earth. There is no divorce, abuse, fear, or brokenness in heaven, so I pray reconciliation, healing, and wholeness to earth. Because there is no sickness in heaven, that is how I prayed over my pregnancy—believing that my daughter would live and thrive. But birth defects still happen in a fallen world, and Goldie went home to be with Jesus because of it.

It's moments like these that every Christian comes to a crossroad in their faith. Will we continue to press forward towards Jesus, using Him and His life of miracles as our example of the Father's will? Or will we take our broken hearts and run, getting bitter and offended when our prayers don't line up with the perfect will of God in heaven? Will we form new theology around our experiences to protect our hearts from disappointment, or will we run into the arms of the Miracle Maker, letting Him teach us who He is and how we can have faith that can move mountains?

These days when things get tough, I am learning to run as fast as I can to sit at the feet of Jesus and hear His voice. And because faith comes from hearing, the more I hear, the more faith I have. The more faith I have, the more I see miracles.

Every time I retreat into His arms and listen to His heart, I am more convinced of His goodness. He reminds me that I'm His child with an inheritance of righteousness, wholeness, freedom, and abundant life. He tells me that I'm filled with the Holy Spirit and empowered to pray and bring His kingdom to earth, as Jesus did. He kisses my face and wipes my tears, assuring me that His plans for me are always good and that I'm constantly on His mind as He intercedes for my life. He encourages me to agree with Him, and not the deceiver, giving heaven the power to release the supernatural in my life.

I don't have the answer to why some prayer requests materialize on this earth and some don't. I don't understand why some people are healed miraculously and some aren't. What I do know is that there is a tumbling ball of pain, sin, death, disease, and destruction that will continue to have power in this fallen world, because that is where we live. But even though my physical body bleeds in its mortality, my spirit is alive with Christ as a citizen of heaven. And I have been commissioned to bring that kingdom to earth.

Ultimately, I have the free will to choose to believe that Jesus is the solution to the brokenness of mankind, or to give up and throw in the towel. My heart has made a conscious choice to run into intimacy, even when things don't work out the way that I prayed they would. The more I know His heart, the more convinced I am that He has always been good, even when the fallen world gets very, very bad.

Friend, stop being surprised when wounded people act wounded; they will continue to hurt you until they are healed. Stop being shocked when poverty, greed, wars, abuse, corruption, and human trafficking exist in our world; they will keep happening as long as human hearts are estranged from Love, refusing to live connected to their Savior and Healer. Stop being indignant when sickness, sin, and death happen in a broken world. As long as your heart remains offended towards God for all the bad things that have happened to you, you will never find peace.

Our God is always faithful to renew life out of death and restore everything that's been lost. Therefore, I implore you, as Paul did to the Corinthians, *be reconciled to God* (2 Corinthians 5:20). Put down the guns that you've aimed at Him in accusation and dare to let Him come close inside of your disappointment. Let Him draw near where you have been beaten to a pulp by life—pulling you in close as the Comforter. Your healing is waiting on the other side of a heart grown bitter, just as mine was that day in front of a black wall of smoke. When I saw that I guarded my heart *from Jesus,* I quickly realized that I had also guarded my heart *from the solution.*

If you're ready to let the medicine of heaven into the heartache that's been infecting your life, then all He needs is a crack of willingness. If you're ready to risk that His goodness and His faithfulness will redeem and restore, all He requires is your permission.

So, beloved, what in the world could you possibly be waiting for?

It's time to be whole.

It's time to be loved.

It's time for every part of your heart to be reconciled to God and set free from the curse of sin and death.

Open-Heart Surgery

1. Take several minutes, close your eyes, and begin to describe how your heart views God. How you see, feel, hear, and experience your heavenly Father. Is He trustworthy or untrustworthy? Is He distant, cruel, and angry, or loving, merciful, and kind? You will relate to God in the way that you perceive Him, so your view of God is essential to uncover before you can move into deeper relationship.

2. Every day, all around the world, God gets blamed for the natural consequences of bad decisions made by humans. What are some of the things you have blamed God for that were the result of your free will? Have you been angry at Him about the consequences of things you've done, ignoring the fact that He didn't come down from heaven and force you to do them?

3. Can you see that the bad decisions of government and church leaders, caretakers, countries and governments, the weather, and family members might be the reasons behind your heart pain, and not because the hand of God was against you? What are some outside factors where

the bad decisions of others have wounded your heart, but God still got the blame?

4. Have there been things in your life that were the result of a fallen world, and not because your good God willed them into existence? Did you pray and believe in accordance with God's Word, yet the miracle didn't manifest and your heart grew cold? Take a few minutes and talk to God about the times you prayed and were disappointed. Did you run from Him, or towards Him? Ask Him to show you *His* perspective of the situation. Is He angry too? Sad? Grieving? What is God's view of you, and what does He want to redeem and restore in your life?

Chapter 5

The Undivided Heart

If you ever get the chance to meet Father Andrew Miller, you will find yourself encountering joy bundled up in a jolly man with a clerical collar. Although his earthly credentials more than qualify him to help people, it's not his twenty-five years as a marriage and family therapist or his title as Anglican priest that enabled him to help set severely wounded people free. Rather, it was his beautiful heart that longed to love people as Christ loved them.

For some reason, the worst of the worst emotional cases kept showing up in his office for therapy sessions—satanic ritual abuse victims, people horribly traumatized who had fragmented into Dissociative Identity Disorder (DID), and those tormented by an unseen realm—feeling and acting more than a little crazy. Even though the world would say he was fully equipped with years of education, spiritual training, and diplomas adorning his office walls, he kept encountering cases that modern psychology—and even Christians—would label as impossible to heal. But when someone is sitting in front of you gushing blood and you claim to believe in a Jesus who promises to heal every wound, you get desperate to find a bandage that works.

When we pray and nothing changes, many times as believers we use the outcome as an occasion to alter our theology to match our experience. When we do this, we stop pressing forward in faith to find out why the natural world didn't line up with what we expected. But in Matthew 17, when the disciples prayed and couldn't get the demon out of the epileptic boy, they didn't form new theology around their failure, deciding it was God's will to heal some and not others. Rather, they brought the boy to Jesus, and he was instantly healed. Jesus' powerful display of His perfect will gave the disciples a lesson in faith and showed them what was available to all of us who press in, mature, and believe.

In the same way, just because every patient coming to Reverend Miller wasn't instantly zapped into wholeness didn't mean he gave up on their broken hearts as they pleaded for help. He began studying, praying, and tirelessly pouring over the Scriptures, determined to find tools that would help his clients know freedom and deliverance from their horrific earthly chains—just like the tortured demoniac in Mark 5 who regained his right mind, completely at peace after encountering the mercy and love of Jesus.

No matter how tattered a heart becomes by the punches of life, Jesus has never encountered an impossible case. He told us we were going to do greater things than even He did—and Andrew Miller believed that promise. After decades of working as a therapist with an emphasis on childhood trauma and clocking in more than 4,000 clinical hours loving on actual broken hearts in sessions, Andrew uncovered a common thread in all of his patients. Every person on the continuum of brokenness had the same primary components within their heart: the *emotional heart*, the *guardian heart*, and the *function heart*.

As God began to reveal and unpack these parts of the heart to Andrew, he started seeing miracle after miracle happen in his counseling practice. The broken and divided hearts of his patients could encounter Someone more powerful than their pain, and as Jesus was allowed access to bind up the pieces, He would sync every part of their hearts back together. Andrew watched person after person find the treasure that the whole world is looking for: wholeness.

God's intention for your heart has always been to bind it up, making it undivided and whole, just as He promised in Ezekiel 11:19: "I will give them an undivided heart and put a new spirit in them; I will remove from them their heart of stone and give them a heart of flesh" (NIV). The glorious Godhead who lives inside you can fuse these three parts of your heart together, giving it the potential to bring forth a fullness of life beyond your wildest dreams.

THE EMOTIONAL HEART

"Behold, my servants shall sing for gladness of the heart, but you shall cry out for pain of heart and shall wait for breaking of spirit."　　　　　　　　　　(Isaiah 65:14 ESV)

When most of us think about the heart, the first thing we probably recognize is our emotions. This emotional heart swoons over a romantic love story and goes weak at the knees when a first love touches our hand. It's the part of us that falls head over heels in love and experiences bursts of joy, but it's also the part that feels as if it was gutted with a hunting knife when we get dumped and recoils in agony when a loved one tells us that we are stupid, ugly, or unwanted. Whether you're conscious of it or not, you know your emotional heart extremely well because it's the part of you most closely connected to your pain.

When I was six years old, I took a few gymnastics classes. Standing in my red leotard, I eyed a class of girls ranging in ages from five to eight, finding the popular crowd before I chose where to sit down on the blue floor mat. As I plopped down right beside the oldest and coolest girl with curly blond hair, she looked over and smiled—my heart exploding with emotions of excitement at her possible friendship.

The class began, and like a puppy following its master, I followed this girl and her two older friends around the gym as we twisted and twirled. Eventually, one by one, we were instructed to make a pass of cartwheels diagonally across the floor, with my spinning legs bringing up the rear. As I ran over to join their little threesome sitting on the floor, they stood up. So I stood up, and they sat down—giggling. I sat down, confused, and once again they stood up laughing, running away, and leaving an emotional heart that felt it had been smashed to bits from their blatant rejection and humiliation.

As you walk through life in a hurtful world with imperfect people, it's impossible for your heart to stay completely safe and unaffected emotionally in some sort of negative way. And when trauma comes like a big school bully who continues to slam you up against the locker, it's normal for your heart to ache terribly. If that ache becomes too great, however, eventually the emotional heart will shut down completely, growing cold in order to survive.

At the end of my eighth-grade basketball season, a team of weepy girls in orange and white hugged and sobbed in the gym as our last practice came to a close. I stood surrounded by peers, longing to cry like them to match the somber mood. But no matter how hard I tried, my eyes stayed dry. My negative emotions had been my enemies for so long that I had shut down *all* of my emotions, growing as hard as stone in self-protection. It was as if someone had filled my heart with cold concrete, and as a result, nothing would leak out of my tear ducts. Feeling that there was something wrong with me for not being an emotional wreck, I snuck away to the utility closet and began to pull out nose hairs, knowing that if I did, I could run back to my friends with watery eyes and pretend to be sad.

In a moment like this, your emotional heart has been so influenced by your unhealed pain that you have formed belief systems around it. One of the greatest and most inaccurate belief systems that I've observed in today's Christian culture is that the emotional heart is so untrustworthy and evil that it must be ignored, crucified, or silenced. Many of us have been taught that the heart and the flesh are the same thing, but they're not. Romans 6:6 makes it clear that "our old sinful selves were crucified with Christ" (NLT), which, plainly put, means that that part of you is dead. Your heart, however, is still alive and inhabited by Christ, making it very silly for you to try to crucify it.

Even when your emotions are negative, they're still valid because they're real, and God wants you to bring them to Him. Your feelings don't just pop out of thin air—there's always a reason behind them. My emotion of fear was the by-product of a life that had proven to be unsafe. My feeling of insecurity was the result of a heart smashed by rejection. My emotion of shame made sense to a heart still dealing with the wounds of sexual abuse.

When you condemn your emotional heart for the normal feelings it produces, both good and bad, instead of trying to understand *why* it feels that way, an essential part of your heart gets stifled and shamed, eventually shutting down to cope. However, your emotional heart was created to be fully alive with Christ. It has developed over a lifetime, but it began at conception. As a baby's body is forming in the womb, its heart is already a spiritual and emotional being, and the baby will cringe when its mother is yelling in anger and relax as she sings lullabies, knowing how to decipher emotion even before its brain is fully formed.

As you grew as a young child, your emotional heart was a quick learner, and it only took one major punch to rob its innocence, convincing your heart that life was unsafe. The next time a painful dodgeball came hurling in, our heart immediately responded the same way our arms rise in sub-conscious deflection.

That is when your *guardian heart* emerged.

THE GUARDIAN HEART

"Guard your heart above all else,
for it determines the course of your life."

(Proverbs 4:23 NLT)

Like an armed guard stationed outside the door of your heart, your inner guardian has been given the task of protecting you, so it lives on high alert looking for enemies—especially if life has proven to have many of them. Its sole purpose is to keep you safe, so your guardian heart will do whatever it needs to accomplish this task. It believes more than anything that your pain must stay separated from your consciousness or you will be too overwhelmed to keep functioning.

As a child whose emotional heart had endured its fair share of rejection over the years, when I would get around a new group of people, my inner guardian had one goal—to avoid more trauma. To accomplish this task, it learned how to flow well with each new group dynamic, reducing my chances of being kicked to the curb. Around a cute guy, my guardian heart would rise up and become his best friend to avoid romantic rejection. Around a catty group of girls who thrived on drama, I would dig up gossip and betray innocent friends for their amusement. Around the most popular kids who partied with drugs and alcohol, I supplied the goods and led the fun. Around a teacher deciding grades, I was the front-row student who knew all the answers. Around a church leader who needed talent, I offered my skilled services to ensure admiration. Whatever was needed to stay accepted or avoid more pain, my guardian heart offered freely—even if it went against my core values.

Because this inner guardian believed it was the only one there to protect me, it developed a guerrilla warfare side that was always ready for a brutal fight. When I first got married in 2007, my poor husband didn't have a clue what he had signed up for. There's a reason that God wants you to put a covenant around your marriage relationship, because when someone gets uncomfortably close to all the dysfunction you've worked a lifetime to hide, really nasty behaviors have a tendency to surface like ugly pimples. My poor little emotional heart had been beaten like an abused animal over the years, and my inner guardian knew how to rise up, ready to bite anyone who got too close.

Most days as a newlywed, I secretly binged on football-player-size portions of food to numb old pain when Luke wasn't looking. I hated myself and felt like a disgusting blob of matter for being unable to conquer my old eating disorder. So when this new husband would say normal things to his new bride, such as, "Babe, you are so beautiful," the poor guy would find himself at war. I'd cite all the reasons why he was wrong, turn a cold shoulder, and behave like a monster in hopes of pushing him away—always trying to protect myself from more rejection. Subconsciously I despised who I was, fully aware of all of my less than beautiful behaviors, so if my guardian heart could just keep him from getting too close to see how much of a mess I was inside, maybe he wouldn't divorce me as I thought I deserved.

When we would get in an argument and I'd reach my capacity to cope with the situation, every time, without fail, my inner guardian would throw up her hands and physically run out of the room, retreating in self-preservation. However, I married a "fixer" who always followed his runaway wife. Instead of feeling loved and fought for, however, I usually felt more like a cornered bull in a china shop. My guardian heart would then pull out the big guns—verbal bullets that aimed for my husband's most vulnerable places, armed with accusations and swinging with threats too cruel to ever repeat. I would scream at the top of my lungs and throw my arms around like a crazy woman, yelling and hitting at him to get away so I could escape.

If you have a wounded emotional heart that stays slashed open, then you will always have a well-developed guardian heart that's working tirelessly to keep you safe from more trauma. But the thing is, when this guardian is not securely connected to Jesus, it's always exhausted from trying to defend you from further damage.

THE FUNCTION HEART

"As he thinks in his heart, so is he."

(Proverbs 23:7 AMP)

In the same way every residential building needs a good property manager, the function portion of your heart proudly holds this title. Your body might be the one to carry out the orders and turn them into actions, but this property manager inside your heart is the part of your will that propels you through life—making the decisions to pay your bills on time, drive to the store and shop, eat meals so you stay nourished, and do the laundry so you don't smell too bad. It's also the part that chooses how you spend your time, with whom you spend that time, and what you do when you get there, making it a powerful and essential part of your daily existence and survival.

When this part of your heart is alive, whole, and connected to Jesus, the works of your hands flourish in abundance from a place of relationship. But when your function heart stays disconnected from God, the result is almost always striving, slaving, performance, and perfectionism.

For most of my life as a believer, I had a very "Christianized" function heart. Every day was spent suppressing my real emotions, shielding them from God in shame as I kept busy with good deeds. I would read my Bible out of religious duty, beating myself up if I missed a day. I would serve tirelessly at church, feeling guilty if I ever skipped a meeting or service. When I struggled with addiction, depression, or cycles of sin, I would stuff down my inner self-hatred to work harder, worship longer, and disciple more people. My emotional heart was such a tangled ball of wounds that in order to survive the embarrassment of what was going on inside, I ran in the opposite direction so that I could function at a very high, very productive level.

But Father didn't want a slave—He wanted a daughter.

After years of high achievement and success, with an impressive resume filled with worldly accolades, in my senior year of college I completely crashed. My emotional heart had carried the heavy pain of unhealed trauma for far too long, and at twenty-one I found myself in deep depression, addicted to substances, petrified with anxiety, and most days, only able to get out of bed for emergencies. The wounds in my emotional heart had piled high over time, as heavy as a pile of bricks, and though I'd done a great job of putting on fake smiles and keeping up appearances, the weight eventually pinned me down to a twin-size dormitory mattress, completely shutting down my ability to function as a human being. I made a desperate phone call to my parents, who immediately pulled me out of college and put me in the safe haven of rehab.

Because the sole goal of our function heart is to keep us moving forward, when it's disconnected from Jesus, its best friend and helper is a word we all know well: *denial*. Like Scarlett O'Hara in the movie *Gone with the Wind*, we know what we must do in order to keep us going in spite of our pain. "Oh, I can't think about that now; I'll go crazy if I do. I'll think about it tomorrow!"

Function heart must remain in denial about emotional pain or it can't do what it needs to do to stay alive, or perform to remain loved and accepted, or climb towards more success and achievement. Which means that the function heart hates anything that threatens to keep it from doing its job—especially negative emotions.

Self-hatred, at its core, is simply a product of the parts of our heart at war with one another. My function heart hated my emotions because they always rose up to interfere with my achievement—and achievement was where I gained my identity and acceptance. My emotional heart also hated my function heart for ignoring it over the years. When I finally got every part of my heart into the hands of Jesus, asking Him to sync them together, a miracle happened.

I signed a cease-fire within, allowing my heart to move from constant war into deep rest.

THE UNDIVIDED HEART

It had only been one week since we cremated our little Goldie, and my world felt like a spinning carnival ride that never ended. I stood in my shower, lights off, scalding water pouring over my head and down my face, knowing that if I didn't connect deeply with my heart, it would most definitely grow cold in order to survive the excruciating pain of death.

With eyes closed, I dialed into the Holy Spirit already living inside, asking the Counselor to help me check in with my heart and see it through His eyes.

Emotional heart, how are you doing? I asked.

Instantly, I saw a picture of myself curled up in a fetal position, wailing, covered in a heavy, white comforter soaked wet with tears and the blood of a broken heart. I knew the blanket was the Holy Spirit, so even though my emotional heart was a mess, it was covered by the Comforter and connected to God.

Guardian heart, how are you?

I saw myself as a warrior being carried by Jesus, dressed in battle armor and gushing blood, wounded and broken. I knew that my guardian heart was connected to Jesus and that my Savior would protect me as I healed. I was right where I needed to be.

Function heart, how are you?

Mimicking a scene from the movie *Talladega Nights*, in which race car driver Ricky Bobby is awkwardly interviewed before his race, I saw my two hands begin slowly to rise up towards my face, and I was unsure of what to do with them. My function heart looked at Jesus and asked the same question that Ricky asked in the movie, "What do I do with my hands?" I burst out laughing through my tears, grateful that I didn't feel obligated to fix myself as I would have in the past, or numb myself with substances or busyness.

As I placed my hands in the hands of Jesus, I knew that every part of my heart—my emotions, my guardian, and my functional heart—was connected to God, and He could bring them back together. I was safe and ready to begin the process of healing.

In the months following Goldie's death, I have learned to check in with my heart thousands of times, making sure it's connected to Jesus. When it's dialed into His presence, it's tuned to peace.

INNER PEACE

The other day as I picked up around my house like a frustrated tornado, my disappointment from a recent betrayal came spewing out in harsh comments. Moses ran into the room and yelled, "Mom, you need inner peace like Kung Fu Panda!" I laughed at my son's reference to the cartoon, grateful for the reminder that inner peace is always available to me, especially with the Prince of Peace living inside.

As long as parts of your heart are at war with one another, the peace you long for will remain beyond your reach. As long as you despise your negative emotions, they can never change. As long as you condemn your old wounds, they will never heal. And as long as you stay in denial, you can never uncover truth and be made whole. The only way for your heart to live in unity with God is if you're also living in unity with yourself. This can happen only if you call in a skilled mediator, Jesus, who sits with all the parts of your heart, both wounded and whole, and begins a safe, truthful, inner conversation in which everything is brought to light and laid out on the table.

It's time to take your lead from the Jesus within, the one who never condemns your heart for being broken. From His example, you will learn the patient art of listening to yourself with grace, accepting without condemnation, empathizing with kindness, and understanding with love as your heart is finally given full permission to do what it must in order to heal.

It must learn to speak freely, knowing it will be heard by Love.

Open-Heart Surgery

1. Close your eyes, take a deep breath of the Holy Spirit, and check in on your emotional heart. What state is this heart in, and what does it look like? Does it feel out of

control with feelings, or shut down and cold in order to survive? Is it wounded, bitter, and angry, or full of joy, peace, and hope? Have you hated this part of your heart for being wounded? What are the normal emotions that this part of your heart produces (e.g., fear, shame, insecurity, anger, or peace, joy, love, acceptance)?

2. Check in with the inner guardian that God gave you to protect your heart. Is this part connected to Jesus, guarding your intimacy with Him, or has it felt as if it needed to protect you from more pain? Have you guarded your pain so you could continue functioning in life? Have you guarded your heart from Jesus in anger or disappointment? Take several moments and ask the Holy Spirit to show you a picture of the guardian portion of your heart. What state is this guardian in? What would it take to keep this part of you connected to Jesus?

3. Check in on the property manager of your heart—the part of you that makes decisions and gets things done. Is this part of your heart on autopilot, getting things done out of duty and necessity, or is it connected to God so that you come alive doing what you were created to do? How much of your Christian life is lived out of function and duty, and how much of your relationship with God involves all of your heart, including your emotions? Ask the Holy Spirit to show you a picture of this part of your heart that gets things done. What does it look like, what condition is it in, and how can it stay connected to Jesus?

4. When every part of your heart is connected to the God who lives inside, abiding in harmony with each other, then your heart will experience deep peace, joy, and abundant life. But if parts of your heart are at war with one another, you will never know peace. Ask the Holy Spirit, once again, to show you a picture of your whole heart. Is your heart at war within? Do you hate your emotions for sabotaging your life, or are your emotions angry for being neglected, silenced, and forgotten? Take a moment and check in with your whole heart, sitting with the Mediator Jesus to have a truthful inner dialogue. When every part of your heart is connected and working together with Jesus, wholehearted living is the result.

Chapter 6

The Languages
of the Heart

As a little third-grader sporting a less-than-flattering
navy-and-white-checkered uniform, I was required
by my private Christian school in Lubbock, Texas, to take
French classes. Although as an adult I might not be able to
remember one word I learned in class that year, I can still
remember almost every part of the French national anthem,
because it was set to music.

As mortifying as it is to admit, I used to walk around
our local mall as an eighth grader, speaking out the words
to that national anthem with different inflections and forming fake sentences—pretending to be a whimsical French
girl lost in a West Texas town. To an untrained Texan's ear,
I might have been able to sound like a fluent Parisian, but in
reality, I could have been talking about chopped liver and
ice cream, and no one would have been the wiser.

Every day, your heart is speaking rather loudly to you,
but until you learn its languages and begin to listen, you
will find yourself living with a foreigner, unable to understand a thing.

Before my son Moses knew how to speak, he definitely knew how to cry—especially while strapped into his car seat. Almost every time we would put infant Moses in the car and head off somewhere, the poor little guy wouldn't just whimper; he would scream as if you were poking him with a hot cattle prod. We tried pacifiers, mirrors, singing, electric toys with buttons, essential oils—you name it, and we gave it a go, trying to help our son enjoy inevitable car rides.

Many times my whole body would tense up from the screams, anxious and frustrated, sending every nerve in my body into high alert. Other times, I would just cry, overwhelmed that I didn't know what to do to soothe my son. There were moments when I'd reach my limit and give in to anger, snapping at him with a harsh tone instead of understanding patience. If I could have understood my son's language, he might have told me that his seat belt was too tight or the position we had him in was uncomfortable for his little frame. He might have expressed how his relational heart felt alone and abandoned in the backseat, wanting someone to be with him just to hold and touch his hand. But because I wasn't fluent in the language of screams, all I could do was guess why he was crying and try to help appease him. Eventually I would get frustrated, over-whelmed, anxious, and exhausted and simply want to avoid the situation altogether.

Friend, this is how a lot of us have treated our extremely loud and sometimes annoying hearts. When our hearts are screaming and we try everything we can to get them to shut up, eventually giving up and avoiding the annoyance altogether, we never find out why they're crying in the first place. And I promise you, just like a baby only cries when there is pain or a substantial need, the heart always has a very valid reason for making noise. When we try to muzzle the symptom, we never uncover the actual problem—which also means we won't ever find a permanent solution.

In Luke 8:8, Jesus said, "Listen with your heart and you will understand!" (TPT). The more I began to pay attention to my heart, the more I began to hear four primary languages that it was speaking, crying, and screaming to try to get my attention. For many years it seemed as though culture, religion, and tradition had encouraged me to ignore the screams as they came spilling out from within, teaching me to bind and gag my inner voices and take care of the annoyance before anyone noticed. I was taught to shame my heart like a loud kid in an uptight church service, hating anything negative that came out. But if you ever want to understand yourself and restore your original design—living as the person God created you to be—then you're going to need to learn to translate a few languages to find out the truth that your heart has been longing to tell you.

As believers, every one of us should live with a central goal for our heart to think, speak, feel, and act in the fluent language of God, *which is the language of love.* But until every part of our heart is flying the unified flag of love above all pain, trauma, bitterness, and offense, it will continue to spew out all sorts of things we would rather it didn't.

If you're like me, your heart has been trying to get your attention for a very long time. So let's give it what it's always wanted by exploring four languages of the heart:

1. The language of **thoughts.**

   "You perceive every movement of my heart and soul,
   and understand my every thought before it even enters
   my mind." (Psalm 139:2 TPT)

2. The language of **words.**

   "For the mouth speaks what the heart is full of."
   (Luke 6:45 NIV)

3. The language of **emotions.**

   "A joyful heart is good medicine."
   (Proverbs 17:22 ESV)

4. The language of **actions.**

   "Do not let my heart incline to any evil,
   to busy myself with wicked deeds."
   (Psalm 141:4 ESV)

So take off your critical lens of judgment and really start to pay attention to your heart through the filter of the counseling—and never condemning—Holy Spirit.

THE LANGUAGE OF THOUGHTS

Standing on green sanctuary steps in my Sunday frills displayed for the entire Methodist church, I belted my little song in unison with the rest of the children's choir.

"Jesus loves me, this I know, for the Bible tells me so!"

As a young preacher's kid with mandatory church several times a week, I knew every word to every Christian sing-along, was up to date with my felt-board Bible stories, and had memorized loads of impressive Scriptures before I knew what most of them meant. Although I might have looked the part while singing songs about God's unconditional love, the little girl on the church steps was dealing with the daily storm that accompanied deep childhood trauma. She didn't always believe the words stored up in her head that came so effortlessly out of her mouth.

My head might have been brimming with knowledge of the gospel truth from years in Sunday school, but my brain was filled with anything but loving thoughts—especially towards myself. In fact, the thoughts tumbling relentlessly through my head were in a brutal war, pitting what I had *learned to be true* against the reality of what I had *experienced to be true*. Though my brain was filled with memorized songs and Scriptures about God's unconditional love, my heart had experienced a perverted love that robbed my innocence.

Unwanted encounters with a sexual world outside of my home had crushed my soul, leaving gaping holes as big as the sun. Because I was so young and didn't have a clue how to deal with the aftermath, my little head was tormented with fear and shame. *Can anyone love me?* My tiny brain would clang with the unconscious, tormenting words on a daily basis. *If anyone knew what happened to me, surely no one would love me.* I was afraid my parents would find out and stop loving me. I was afraid I was too dirty to ever be clean. I was afraid I would always be damaged goods. Because I had been a victim of sexual trauma, my wounded heart believed I was a victim—so I thought like a victim.

The head might know, but it's the heart that believes. And your thoughts don't mirror what you've learned as fact as much as they expose what you've come to believe through experience. The thoughts that pop into your head don't just appear out of thin air; many of them grow out of the central source of your core beliefs—your heart. This is why your attempts to simply wrangle your negative, painful thoughts to the ground and just change your thinking patterns haven't always worked the way you have wanted them to.

Because I was a young twenty-something songwriter fresh out of rehab from an eating disorder, the New York City streets around my Manhattan apartment provided creativity with endless bursts of inspiration, but also with hopeless torment. I would make eye contact on the street with the perfection of a size zero model gliding past me as if on a catwalk in Paris, and my thoughts would claw at my heart with feelings of inadequacy. It was as if a monster had crawled into my brain and begun to chew on all my wires, and no matter what I tried, I couldn't get the beast of comparison to leave. I would memorize Scriptures like the one in 2 Corinthians 10:5, where Paul urges us to fight with our weapons that are not of this world.

> "On the contrary, they [these weapons] have divine power to demolish strongholds. We demolish arguments and every pretension that sets itself up against the knowledge of God, and we take captive every thought to make it obedient to Christ." *(2 Corinthians 10:4–5 NIV)*

The instant I would become aware of a negative thought, I would envision myself attacking and binding the monster in my head, then kicking him out of my skull and declaring Scripture about how I didn't have to be a supermodel because I was fearfully and wonderfully made. But every time I would finish my thought-wrangling routine, I would turn the corner, only to find another gorgeous model, and I would have to repeat the whole exhausting process over and over and over again.

You see, the verse I had memorized only worked to get rid of negative thoughts if I understood the difference between a stronghold and an argument—and at that point, I didn't.

An *argument* is a lie, and we can learn to take those thoughts captive quickly before they make their way into our hearts. But the more you listen to an argument, siding with the "facts," the more power you give them. *Strongholds* are lies that have already worked their way into your core, where you believe them to be concrete truth. I believed myself to be inferior to perfect models. I believed myself to be damaged on the inside unless I could be perfect on the outside. In order for my thoughts ever to change, I had to get to the core and take on what had become a stronghold within my heart.

After years of beating my head against a wall, trying to convince my brain of all sorts of things that my heart didn't yet believe (like the fact that I was lovable, beautiful, capable, pure, whole, and free), Father had me take a step back to look at the situation from another perspective: His. And He was smiling while gazing into my broken heart, seeing a place of amazing potential for miracles rather than a hopeless mess beyond repair.

When I would think about how ugly I was, instead of shaming myself for the thought, I would practice taking my mind and heart straight to Jesus and putting them into His hands, being honest with Him about how I really felt through confession. I would close my eyes and watch as He would pull me in close with such kindness, whispering how He was crucified once so that I didn't have to keep crucifying myself. When I found myself dwelling in a funk about how unlovable I was, instead of berating myself with disgust, I would let Jesus put His hand directly on the wound, imparting His loving thoughts about me that outnumbered the grains of the sand.

"Christa . . ." I'd close my eyes and listen as His voice whispered sweetly to my spirit. "You're the most beautiful thing I've ever seen—and you are all mine. When I look at you, beloved, my heart explodes. When I see you smile, I dance and sing wildly with joy. You have captured my heart, my prized love, and being with you is my favorite thing in the universe" (Zephaniah 3:17 paraphrased).

Instead of hating my negative head, I started using it to my advantage. Instead of condemning my bad thoughts, I began using them as pathways towards a heart encounter with a very real person named Jesus—the One always ready to tell me the beautiful truth.

THE LANGUAGE OF WORDS

"Oh man, my hair looks just awful."

I huffed and puffed in front of the bathroom mirror, frustrated that nothing in the beauty department seemed to be cooperating that day. My jeans weren't buttoning up without squishing out a muffin top over my waistline, my face had broken out, and to top it all off, I had forgotten to do a load of laundry and had run out of clean undies.

Just awesome.

"Babe," my husband said softly from the next sink over, spitting out a mouthful of toothpaste, "do you have any idea how negative you are when you stand in front of the mirror?"

"I'm not *that* negative," I snapped back in quick defense, letting out a frustrated sigh. "I'm just having a bad reflection day."

Turning to walk back into the bedroom, Luke stopped for a moment and looked over his shoulder. "You should start listening to yourself when you're getting ready, Christa. I think you'd be really surprised at what you hear."

Years ago, when I decided to take my wise husband's advice and start paying attention to my speech, I wasn't just alarmed at what was coming out when I was standing in front of the mirror—I was surprised at how negative I was the majority of the time. I would leave a church service and immediately become an expert judge—critiquing the sermon, worship leader, music choices, theology—weighing in about all the things I would do differently and, of course, better. I'd get around someone who wanted to process their recent betrayal, but instead of empathizing and offering sound solutions, I would use it as an opportunity to spew out all the times I, too, had been stabbed in the back, continuing to stir our mutually bitter pot. Someone would reveal a secret they weren't supposed to tell, so I'd uncover something I had sworn would never leave my lips in a moment of negative bonding. When I found myself around an important person I wanted to impress, I would keep interjecting and steering the conversation towards my impressive achievements in an attempt to make myself look better.

The overflow of my mouth was a toxic waste dump of vent sessions, opinions, judgments, and pointless information that never did anything but perpetuate all sorts of poisonous problems. And most days, I would crawl up on the judgment seat of my life, looking down to critique myself and others with harsh tones and perfectionistic standards, letting the words spray out like bullets.

At times, I would feel true sorrow and deep remorse for a gossip session or negative rant, and I'd swear before God to change my ways. I would memorize Scriptures like the one in Psalm 141:3, pleading with Father to, "Set a guard, O Lord, over my mouth; keep watch over the door of my lips!" (ESV). Or to prove to God my devotion to change, I would put money into a "Negativity Jar" on my bedside table every time my mouth decided to spew out something less than pure.

But trying to put tape over an active geyser does very little to shut down the explosion beneath the earth, just as taping up a mouth does nothing to change the cesspool inside the heart. The heart must change before the overflowing speech will.

The thing is, bad speech doesn't have to be a total waste of breath, as I used to believe. In fact, if you start paying attention to your words without shame and condemnation, under the kind tutelage of a counseling Holy Spirit, you can pretty much pinpoint all sorts of secret rooms that Jesus needs to be invited into. And instead of focusing solely on muzzling your mouth or striving tirelessly to alter your bad speech, you find that God has been waiting to heal the hurt behind the words, gently pulling out old lies and replacing them with the truth.

The other day, a new girlfriend brought up a pastor who had betrayed me over a decade ago, and before I was conscious of what I was doing, my mouth started spewing out little jabs and justifying them as "warnings" to keep her from getting hurt. But since "love covers over a multitude of sins" (1 Peter 4:8 NIV), I realized that the words coming out of my mouth revealed a heart that hadn't yet forgiven. Instead of trying to will away the pain of that betrayal and force myself to forgive a man who had smashed up my heart, I took my broken heart (and my anger and unforgiveness) to Jesus, confessing the reality of the situation and placing it all in His hands.

As I asked Jesus to heal the wound of that betrayal, His presence filled me with such empathy and grace for that pastor that I could feel the wound closing up within, releasing true forgiveness. For the first time in over a decade, I can honestly say that if I saw that man, I would genuinely hug him without bitterness—and my negative speech played a huge part in uncovering my festering heart so it could heal.

Whenever I'm late for an event and start to get snappy

and bossy around my family during the final house roundup, I stop, take a deep breath, and confess the truth: "God, my frustrated words are revealing my true heart." Then, instead of condemning myself, I end up thanking my heart for telling me that I still have wounds of fear that make me want to control the uncontrollable. If I'm in front of the mirror and begin to verbally assault my reflection, I close my eyes, put my hand on my chest, and sigh deeply, grateful that my heart is crying out so loudly that I can clearly hear that it still bears wounds from rejection.

Plain and simple, all negative speech points to a deeper need for the heart to be sanctified. So instead of being cruel to your heart for its brutal honestly, take a moment and express gratitude, thanking it for speaking so loudly. At its core, it's still a beautiful work in progress, in need of a miracle-working Savior.

THE LANGUAGE OF FEELINGS

I sat down to prepare my message for a conference in New York City, where I had been invited to speak alongside one of my favorite speakers and mentors, Lisa Bevere. As I sat with Father in preparation for the event, letting my personal creativity swirl in unison with the Holy Spirit guiding me from within, I started getting excited about the sermon He was pulling out of my heart as it began to pour onto the pages of my notes.

Oh man, this is going to make me look really good in front of Lisa! The random feelings of insecurity would hit my body like electricity, and I would bat them away like an annoying fly, embarrassed that they kept buzzing around at all. But before long, I would find myself envisioning Lisa sitting on the front row as I spoke, and overwhelming emotions would tumble through my being in the form of sentences. *I hope she likes me more after she hears this message. In fact, this sermon will make me look really wise and spiritual, which has to gain me some brownie points in her eyes.*

As if waking up from a silly daydream, I quickly shook my head back and forth to reenter reality, confused by the overwhelming emotions of inadequacy seeping like poison from my heart.

Old Christa would have immediately started whipping herself for feeling so ridiculous, rebuking the negative emotions, declaring Scripture about my identity being in Christ (and not in the opinions of Lisa Bevere), and taking authority over the supposed onslaught of the enemy. I'd then inevitably move into deep self-condemnation for being such a people pleaser and call it the conviction of the Holy Spirit. But the new Christa—the one who was learning to approach her heart very differently—began to do something different.

I asked my heart a simple question, *Heart, what are you trying to tell me, dear friend?*

As I tuned my attention like a radio to listen to my feelings of inadequacy, bringing them into the light and confessing them in repentance before Father *without shame*, He began to displace the situation on center stage and help me decipher the insecurity that had eaten at me for decades.

My daddy always says that children can be great recorders, but sometimes terrible interpreters. My little girl heart interpreted that when my baby brother came home from the hospital, my mother abandoned me. Because of this interpretation, my heart always longed for nurture from female figures, and something deep within strived for women's affirmation. When I didn't feel like I got what I needed, I developed a deep insecurity and a need to perform around women I admired and respected. As I prayed with Jesus that day on the plane taking me to New York, I felt like the little girl who had felt all alone for a very long time, and I collapsed into His arms for a good cry.

Thank you, heart, I whispered deep inside that day on the airplane. *Thank you for showing me how you need a touch from Jesus inside these old painful feelings that have chased me into my adult years. God, I know you as Father, but I need to know the nurturing nature of your feminine heart—because in Isaiah 66:13 you tell me, "As a mother comforts her child, so will I comfort you" (NIV). I give you permission to bind up old wounds of insecurity and rejection. Thank You for being both male and female and giving me the best of both as You nurse this broken place within me back to health.*

If I had simply ignored my people-pleasing thoughts that day in preparation for my message, quoted Scripture at it, or tried to suppress the insecurity twisting like a thorny weed out of my heart, I promise you, those feelings would have returned again, and again, and again—around every important female who crossed my path. But as I listened with patience, I finally heard. As I heard with kindness, I finally understood. And because I finally understood, every time emotions rose up and I surrendered them into His hands, Jesus continued to restore those broken places and make my heart whole.

THE LANGUAGE OF ACTIONS

With tears pouring like waterfalls down my already reddened face, I shoveled handfuls of chips into my mouth with both hands, barely chewing before swallowing hard, only to repeat the act all over again.

Why are you doing this, Christa? I would scream, sob, and plead with my physical body to stop the overeating binge of sometimes 5–10,000 calories in one sitting. But the pain in my broken heart was determined to be numbed by a medicating food addiction, no matter the cost.

You see, addictions and compulsions are never about just behaviors or substances. They're about a broken heart that can't handle any more pain. After every time I'd binge, I would write out a detailed plan in my journal of all the things I was going to do to manage my eating disorder, change my bad behaviors, and eliminate this devouring monster from my life. I would pledge to stick to my meal plan and write out my menus, obeying my nutritionist and working out my body to eliminate the unwanted pounds—always repenting to God in shame for being so weak and disgusting.

But because the core pain that caused the addiction was rarely acknowledged, I never found freedom by simply controlling my behavior. I might have had a good day here and there, or possibly even found myself able to muster up enough self-restraint to manage food for an entire week. But the compulsive acts always came back like ghosts that haunted the halls of my heart, rising up to destroy my life.

Because food is the Christian drug, and there are millions of believers all over the world using this substance to medicate heart pain, people ask me all the time, "Christa, how in the world did you get free from your addiction to food?" Although I can't pinpoint the exact moment when I stopped trying to control and hide the wounded, compulsive, and embarrassing tenants in my heart that led to many addictive behaviors, I can tell you what happened when I shifted my focus from the problem to the solution—handing my master key to an able healer named Jesus. Basically, I turned my eyes away from the food and put my focus on Jesus—the Bread of Life. As I committed to letting Him walk into every shameful room inside to nourish, purify, and heal, the actions growing out of my woundedness began to change naturally from acting out to remaining stable as I faced my heart pain.

I wholeheartedly believe that the current Western church is exhausted and frustrated with their sanctification strategy because a lot of it is aimed at correcting all the things we can see, instead of letting the Holy Spirit search our hearts, know us, try us, and heal us from the inside-out. As a result, a huge majority of us have battled depression, anger, disappointment, judgment, fear, addictions, and self-loathing, frustrated because we can't will ourselves to change. We have learned from rejection to keep our shame hidden behind closed doors so we don't lose our ministry platforms. Droves of Christians are hiding secret sins, addictions, and struggles, because many of us are taught to manage our symptoms without letting God heal the reasons behind them.

Yet, when we aim at our symptoms, hacking away with our own strength at impure thoughts, negative words, embarrassing emotions, and bad behaviors, we might experience temporary change through self-restraint, but never permanent freedom. The prophet Jeremiah writes,

> "The heart is hopelessly dark and deceitful,
> a puzzle that no one can figure out.
> But I, GOD, search the heart
> and examine the mind.
> I get to the heart of the human.
> I get to the root of things.
> I treat them as they really are,
> not as they pretend to be."
>
> *(Jeremiah 17:9–10 MSG)*

No matter how dedicated you are, how hard you strive, or how strong you become, you will never possess the power to heal, cleanse, and purify the brokenness inside your heart *because this has never been your job.* Your role in life is to be a much-loved child, receiving all that Father offers through salvation, and letting Him complete His work in you through an exchange of supernatural power and relationship.

For me, becoming free of addictions, shame, fear, and the painful feelings that triggered them has taken time, and to this day I still need oceans of empowering grace for the process of sanctification in many areas. Now, because Jesus is healing my heart, if I'm being harsh and controlling with my family, I stop, thank my heart for speaking loudly to get my attention, and confess that I must still be filled with anger and frustration with myself. If I'm being unkind and impatient with others, I use it as an indicator that I'm probably not being very kind or patient with myself. Whatever is spewing out in my actions reveals the contents of my heart, showing me what I need to receive from Father.

These days, instead of working hard to behave correctly and remain sinless, I take my focus off of all I'm doing wrong, and instead focus on all He's doing right. I draw close to Jesus and ask Him to show me what true intimacy looks like in my deepest parts. As I begin to eat and drink of His Word, Spirit, character, and love, my inner world pours out into my outer world, and my actions become a beautiful reflection of what a supernatural God is doing inside my heart.

Listen to the heart God gave you today, beautiful friend. Listen with grace like He does, and you will understand. Watch to see what kinds of thoughts, words, emotions, and actions are residing in your heart. And instead of swinging an axe at your sin and struggling in the name of devotion to God, instead, why don't you hand the axe over to Him and see what He wants to do? I have a feeling He wants to teach you to listen as He hears, see as He sees, and understand as He does—with grace, compassion, and unconditional love.

Open-Heart Surgery

1. Our hearts tend to be the place we most neglect. If your heart has always been speaking to you, and you haven't known how to listen, then take a few moments and simply apologize. Apologize to your heart for ignoring it, neglecting it, or for not knowing how to handle its cries.

2. If your heart is the source of your thoughts, then consider what your thoughts are like. Do they tend to be negative or positive, tormenting or affirming? Instead of condemning your thoughts, or quoting Scripture at them to try to make them change, take a few minutes, close your eyes, and thank your heart for speaking so loudly to you. Ask the Holy Spirit to begin tracing negative thoughts back to specific wounds in your heart, giving you an encounter with His presence that heals the wound inside.

3. Out of the overflow of the heart, the mouth speaks. So what are you saying that reveals your heart? Take a moment and thank your heart, removing the self-condemnation. Find five things you consistently say that you wish you didn't, and ask the Holy Spirit to trace those words or phrases back into your broken heart, revealing the source. Now, stop and ask God for an *encounter* with Him within that situation, binding up your broken heart so free speech can flow.

4. Your emotions are not your enemies, and they're not bad—they simply reveal the content and condition of your heart. Take a deep breath, giving yourself permission to feel. Ask the Holy Spirit to take your walls down,

allowing you to become conscious of what your heart is truly feeling. As emotions begin to arise, just sit with them. Don't try to change them. Just accept them, even if you want them to change. Now, thank your heart for being honest, and ask the Holy Spirit to help you trace those emotions back to wounded roots. Take some time to *be with Jesus* inside of your emotions, knowing that He can handle them all.

5. Our actions reveal what's going on inside more than anything, which is why it's pointless to try to change the action without changing the heart. With the Holy Spirit, take inventory of your actions, both positive and negative. Without shame, begin to trace your actions back to the heart, asking Father to meet you inside of every wound. If you struggle with addiction, then thank your heart for screaming loudly, and ask the Holy Spirit to get to the root. If you're battling compulsions, sexual sin, anger, or lethargy, then accept your actions as the result of brokenness, and ask Father to meet you inside your heart. Make this a lifestyle, and not an encounter. Make this your intention each day.

Chapter 7

The Naked Heart

As my husband turned up the volume on our television set, his efforts to drown out the lawn mower next door did little to drown out the worried thoughts screaming inside my newlywed head.

For years, I had been a touring musician, traveling the world and playing with all sorts of artists, the most recent being Christian music legend Michael W. Smith. In an attempt for me to be a newly married girl who wasn't leaving on a tour bus every few days, we made the decision for me to quit traveling to enjoy my newly married situation. But with neither of us bringing in steady income, our choice also left us enjoying an old upstairs apartment with low ceilings, a collection of donated furniture, bright pink carpet that reeked of cigarette smoke from the tenant downstairs, stacks of unpaid bills, and a kitchen stocked with packets of ramen noodles.

That day, as I cuddled up to my fabulous, but very broke new husband on our secondhand couch, the strength of his arms around me wasn't making the anxiety of our present financial situation go away. Before I was even conscious of the downward spiral, questions about our unknown future had infected my heart like a plague, and I found my thoughts overtaken by very real, very crippling fear.

What if we can't pay rent this month?

What if our only car goes on the brink?

What if our cell phones get shut off?

What if I don't start touring again . . . will we be able to eat this month?

"Babe," I said with a forced smile, "I'm just going to run to the bathroom for a minute."

I lifted his arm off of my shoulder and stood, acting like I was headed back to the loo, but making a quick detour into our little kitchen. With years of practice sneaking food to medicate the pain inside my heart, I quietly opened the fridge and began my usual overeating routine, devouring anything and everything I could. We didn't have much in stock, but whatever we had I was going to destroy as fast as I could before returning to his unsuspecting arms, acting as if nothing had happened.

When Luke married me, he knew I had struggled with an eating disorder for most of my life. He knew I had been admitted to inpatient treatment and had years of counseling under my belt. He even knew that when the pain of life became uncontrollable, sometimes food was the one thing I still attempted to control. Every once in a blue moon, I'd finally let Luke in and confess a bingeing episode, long after the binge was over with. But most times, I was far too embarrassed about my behavior to fully disclose all the ugly details to my husband.

As I shoved an oversize bite of leftovers into my mouth, noodles still hanging out and dripping down my chin,

I suddenly froze. Someone was behind me. Someone was watching me. Someone was seeing my shame—the thing that made me completely unlovable, or so I believed.

I turned around slowly, dreading the look of disgust I was sure to see, the judgment, the fury of hatred—the same hatred I had for myself. But far from condemnation, this new husband of mine had something on his face that I would never have expected: he was looking at me the same way he did on our wedding day.

Pulling himself up backwards onto the countertop and popping open a bag of chips, Luke looked into my eyes with the very love I'd experienced when we made our vows to one another. He looked at this bingeing wife with the same affection as when he had looked at his spotless bride dressed in white.

"Baby," he said quietly with tears beginning to pool inside eyes filled with love. "If you need to binge, I'm going to binge with you. I don't want you to have to do it alone ever again."

In that one earth-shattering moment, the scope of true intimacy was unveiled to my heart. I was being seen in my nasty, addicted, disgusting moment and loved anyway. I was being given the opportunity to be completely naked in front of someone—physically, emotionally, and spiritually. And even though I had always been petrified of anyone looking at all the ugly parts of my life, here was a man who not only saw the mess, but wanted to crawl down in the pit *with* me so I wouldn't have to be alone in the pain.

I have never met a healthy person who thrived and came alive under the heavy chains of rejection, abandonment, abuse, and isolation. I have never met a baby who preferred to be starved, screamed at, and left alone in a soiled diaper to cry out in need or pain. Each person on planet earth was created in the image of Love, which also means we all need to *experience* love in order to thrive and come alive. If you poured soda into your car instead of gasoline, I have a feeling it wouldn't run for very long. If your human heart doesn't receive the love and affection it was made for, your entire being won't run the way it should.

Something healed inside my heart that day when I stood completely exposed in front of my husband, uncovered in the shame of my food addiction. Instead of rejecting me as I had feared—instead of yelling at, judging, or condemning me—he had done the exact opposite. Luke crawled down inside of my dirty pigpen to sit down, kiss my shameful wounds, and commit to stay near and close—even if I never changed. He acted like Jesus, who never pushes the broken away but instead pulls them in closer *because* they're broken and ashamed, knowing that love is the only medicine that covers and heals the naked heart.

TRUE LOVE DRAWS CLOSER

The world we were born into is based on a conditional love system in which affection and promotion are based on external factors. We learn from a very young age that in order to stay close without getting pushed away, we need to do and be more than what we already are. *If* you look a certain way, then I'll love you. *If* you act a certain way, then we can be friends.

But *if* you betray me, then forget about it. *If* you have a certain degree, then I'll hire you. *If* you continue to do well, then you can get promoted. But *if* you don't, you're fired. So many of us are petrified of being less than perfect, because if we're not spotless, experience has taught us that we'll get rejected in a conditional world. Fortunately, God's love is never offered with an agenda, the same way my husband's love for me wasn't given to manipulate my behaviors into healing.

Love loves for the sake of loving.

Over the years, I have encountered scores of exhausted Christians who have reduced God to a distant deity into whom they pour their lives, but rarely stop to let Him pour life into them. They read their Bibles to find out all they're supposed to do in service instead of reading Scripture to experience all that the living Word has done (and is doing) for them. We've grown comfortable living on earth while He's apparently far off into the sky as we sing our three worship songs on a Sunday morning and call it an encounter. We stand in churches full of hands busy with dutiful works, rarely making corporate space to sit at the feet of Jesus as Mary did, learning to listen, receive, and commune intimately with Love.

Before my experience with Jesus in my diamond cave, I had clocked thousands of hours studying, sitting in church meetings, conferences, and worship services over the years, and could easily talk about the library of information about God that I had filed in my brain. I had stuffed my head with sermons, Scriptures, Bible studies, worship songs, precepts, and principles about Jesus, God, and the Holy Spirit—discipled to love, serve, pray, and worship. But if I'm completely honest, the amount of time I've been taught *about God* to my head and *how to serve Him* with my hands is about the size of an ocean compared to the amount of time I've been led to *intentionally encounter Him* as a real person—One who knows and loves me the way that I can know and love Him. One I can taste, see, feel, hear, and experience in my everyday life.

The dictionary defines intimacy as "close familiarity or friendship; closeness." It has also been defined as "In-To-Me-See"—the good, the bad, the beautiful, and the ugly. The apostle Paul wrote to the Corinthians, "The amazing grace of the Master, Jesus Christ, the extravagant love of God, the *intimate friendship of the Holy Spirit*, be with all of you" (2 Corinthians 13:14 MSG, italics mine). God permanently entwined our spirits, souls, minds, and bodies with His indwelling presence so we can have the intimate relationship with Him that we were made for.

When Luke and I had been married for a few years, we felt a burning desire to create children out of the love we already shared, birthing humans in our image and with our DNA. We didn't do it because we wanted workers around the house to help with chores. I didn't get pregnant because we hoped our kids would grow up to help us achieve our dreams. We didn't expand our family so we could raise little people who could tell us how amazing we were all the time. We wanted a family because our hearts yearned to love, know, fellowship, and simply *be with the kids we created*—no matter how they behave.

Out of the love that the Trinity had for one another, they wanted to expand the reach of their intimacy and start a family. God's ultimate goal when He created Adam and Eve in the garden was always true, naked, exposed, intimate relationship with His kids, and it was always His ultimate goal as well when He partnered with your parents' decision to create you.

He wants you because He wants you because He wants you.

When Scripture invites us to experience the amazing grace, extravagant love, and intimate friendship that the Trinity offers, God isn't proposing a distant relationship in which we encounter Him once a week in a church service, or even one hour a day during a quiet time. In fact, the separation theology in our worship songs and churches is sometimes enough to make my blood boil with righteous anger. Do we think that God isn't around until we sing loudly, remain sinless, or pray hard enough to coax Him down from His throne in heaven? The heavens have been forever opened and the veil torn! We have to quit begging the Spirit of God to come close where Jesus bled to remain. God invites us all into intimate connection, where everything is seen and always loved, even when we don't deserve it.

Moreover, God doesn't just love—He actually *is* love. So if the substance of Love is already residing inside of you, then how could you possibly be in a love-deficit ever again? The trick isn't learning to acquire or earn God's love; the trick is learning how to tune in and experience *what's already there*.

The more I learned about the human heart and how it's created to need love and affection, the more I began living to stay plugged into the continual source of love that already lives inside of me—knowing I can only give out what I have first received (1 John 4:19). In fact, I stopped living to love and serve God and, instead, started living to be loved *by Him*. As my heart expands to make room for the abundance of that love available in Christ, I find that oceans of grace start pouring out when I'm in front of people who act like they're in a love-drought. These days when I flip on the news or click on the Internet, hearing yet another report of a shooting, rape, murder, or betrayal, an abuser, cheating pastor, or dirty politician, I don't shake my head in condemning disbelief anymore. My heart can't help but cry for those who clearly don't know how fiercely they are wanted, chosen, and adored. A heart that doesn't believe it's worthy of love tends to act unlovable—in desperate need of a Savior.

LOVE SAVES

People always tell me I'm brave, standing on stage to unveil my less than stellar past and writing about my failures, even as I'm wading through the process. But the thing is, I only find true freedom when I bring every part of my heart into the light, letting unconditional love pour water onto the destructive fires of shame and fear.

True intimacy can be scary to a human heart accustomed to rejection, because it can't have any secrets, coverings, or barriers. But when you finally jump over your fear and unzip your chest, exposing the good and the bad, you find yourself living exposed and receptive to unconditional Love. And love heals everything through intimacy.

God made this intimate relationship with you possible

by introducing a radical new kingdom that turns logic on its head—bringing you into permanent unity with a Love who promises never to leave you or forsake you, and showing you that nothing you can ever do will separate you from His love. This unconditional love system isn't something that can ever be rationalized with logic, because no matter how many angles you approach it from, it will never make any earthly sense.

If you asked me ten years ago what salvation is, I would have spouted off a Sunday school answer about praying a prayer and asking God to forgive my sins. And then to show Jesus how grateful I was for His dying for me, I needed to hand over my life to God in service and stop sinning in exchange for a ticket to heaven. But salvation is so much juicier and tastier than that simple answer that I can't figure out how the whole world doesn't want to sink their teeth in and take a bite. I wonder if that's because some in our Christian culture have reduced salvation to its lowest level. To believe that God has forgiven our sins just so we can have a ticket to heaven someday, all the while painfully enduring constant hell on earth, is simply ludicrous. Especially when we learn what the Greek word for salvation—*sozo*—really means.

The word *sozo* is used over a hundred times in the New Testament, and we usually refer to it as "save" or "saved." But the same word used to describe the forgiveness of sins was also used when Jesus was raising the little girl from the dead in Mark 5:23, when He was casting out devils in the demoniac in Luke 8:36, and when the woman who touched His cloak was physically healed in Matthew 9:22. Jesus came to save us from sin—yes! But He came to do this by delivering and healing our entire being. Having our sins for-given is definitely the centerpiece of salvation—and for that I'm eternally grateful! Yet Jesus suffered and died to bring us much, much more. He died to free us from all sickness, disease, poverty, and depression on this earth. And that's a really big deal.

In Galatians 1:3, when Paul releases a blessing to the church, he prays for them to have "God's undeserved kind-ness and total well-being that flows from our Father-God and from the Lord Jesus" (TPT). The phrase *total well-being* used here is the same word for *peace* used in the Hebraic mind-set that literally means "health, prosperity, peace, and total well-being."

It is the purpose of God, through salvation, that you live in total well-being, or *shalom*—spirit, soul, and body. Through the blood of Christ, a relationship has been made available by which you literally have access to a God who offers peace, health, abundance, and divine wholeness. God doesn't want you to be connected to Him because He's a narcissist who needs constant worship. Instead, He's an adoring Father who knows that the best thing for you is *His love*. God doesn't want you to seek after Him with all of your heart because He's insecure and needs attention; He wants to restore everything in your life that exists at a deficit, over-flowing your being with eternal abundance.

Salvation takes the ugly blackness of an old nature dis-eased with sin that destroys the soul and infuses the life of a perfect Christ into the heart's depravity, miraculously weaving them into a glorious new creation. It takes every coping mechanism, deep wound, old pain, and negative effect of life in the darkness of a fallen world and pumps the heart full of electric light to empower, resurrect, revive, and restore from the inside out. The moment you say yes to Jesus, the barren land of your brokenness is miraculously transformed into a heavenly oasis of eternal medicine. It's the place where all of your pain collides with a Healer ready to bind up every wound. The hell on earth that you've endured under the reign of death is put to an end when the kingdom of abundance is alive inside.

Salvation means that when you look at pornography, the purity of love pulls you in closer to remind you that you're already washed clean. It means that when you're running to food, drugs, sex, alcohol, or substances to numb the pain, Jesus is right there to save time and again, interceding on your behalf with purposeful affection. Grace means that every time you gossip, cheat, lie, hate, or lash out in anger, the Helper rises up in your defense to remind you who you are and who He is, empowering you to overcome and live differently.

In this new kingdom system, anyone can be pardoned for anything because the blood of Jesus seems too good to be true, but actually is true. True love keeps no record of wrongdoings, even when those bad behaviors destroy lives. Somehow, our God is able to remove our sins as far as the east is from the west, wiping us clean and choosing to forget all of our transgressions, not relating to us on the basis of our sins, but on the righteousness of Christ Jesus (Colossians 2:14).

You are His beloved child, and the Trinity proved they would do anything for you when they sent Jesus. Your Father watched in agony while the fallen world bombed your heart with pain, so He devised a plan before time began to overcome the sin and death that keep you locked in chains. Father didn't just have plans to walk *with* you—He wanted to get His hands directly *on* the ruined parts of your heart and set up a home inside the mess, rolling up His sleeves to begin the joy of heart transformation.

Because of salvation, you will never again face a problem alone. The almighty God, the solution for everything, has unpacked His bags and made His permanent home inside, giving you endless access to His perspective, wisdom, counsel, comfort, power, and grace.

All the years of managing dysfunction, patching leaky pipes in your heart, working overtime to perform and hide, and slaving to fix yourself—those years are now over. Now you get to learn how to sink into a free inheritance called peace. A force so powerful that it conquered sin and death has now walked through the door of your life, marked you with His Spirit, and is never, ever, ever leaving or abandoning you—no matter how ridiculous you act.

When God looks at you in your nakedness, He doesn't see all of your blemishes—*He sees Jesus.* As author and speaker Graham Cooke taught me, the Father hid you in the safest place He could think of, concealing you safely into a perfect Christ. In fact, you're no longer allowed to refer to yourself as a sinner, especially since your sin nature has been crucified and you have become a new creation (Colossians 2:12).

Why would a beautiful butterfly keep calling itself a caterpillar just because its feet still touch the ground? You might have temporary moments of memory loss where you forget that you have been transformed into that new butterfly—that you're loved, free, righteous, and forgiven. You might let old wounds produce sinful, unlovable behavior. But it's not who you are anymore, even if you forget and act like your old self. And God never abandons or condemns you when you forget. Instead, He draws close in your weakness, staying near and intimate within relationship to encourage and empower your deeper transformation.

MOVING FROM THE HEAD TO THE HEART

For decades I felt abandoned and estranged from God's presence—especially when I binged on food, lied, messed up, or struggled sexually. I didn't understand that while I could never be separated from the love of God in Christ, it was up to me to keep my heart dialed in and engaged with that love. As Cooke so eloquently puts it, "Relationship is God's responsibility—and He secured that with the cross. But now, fellowship is your responsibility."

Years ago, when I first met the man who would be my future husband, if I had asked Luke to write out information about himself so that I could study, read, and memorize instead of going on dates with the guy, I have a feeling we wouldn't have ended up at the altar. On paper, Luke was a college dropout without a job, no car (only a motorcycle), who liked to climb trees, play his guitar for hours, and hike in the woods to pray and connect with Jesus every day. On top of that, he lived in a house with nine college guys, which made me feel old, since I had been out of school for seven years.

But the more I *experienced* the way his blue eyes looked

at me day in and day out as if he had won the lottery, my heart was quickly stolen away from my brain, abandoning all the silly lists I made about my future soul mate. Luke consistently fought to win my heart like a knight jousting tirelessly in a tournament, and though my mind was first filled with reservation, my heart quickly became certain that he was my life partner. Luke hadn't racked up his earthly credentials like I thought I wanted—he had been too busy on his knees searching out the heart of God. Yet the guy ran after me with such fiercely devoted love, my thirsty soul drank up his affection.

Heart experience trumps head knowledge every time. You might know *about* someone because you've read their biography, but you *believe and trust them* because you have history with them. And that requires intimate relationship. It's easy to open a Bible and read a Scripture with your physical eyes and memorize a sentence with your head, but studying the Bible without *experiencing* the God of the Bible is a total waste of time. If your pursuit of Scripture isn't leading you to intimate fellowship with God, then you've completely missed the mark.

As a woman living in the twenty-first century with access to modern conveniences such as the printing press, podcasts, Bible Gateway searches, concordances, and one-click Amazon book shopping, no one appreciates easy access to the Bible more than I do. The written word of God is better than gold—feeding, nourishing, instructing, and healing my heart on a daily basis as I encounter a real God who breathes life into each word.

At the same time, we have to remember that for the

majority of the two thousand years that Christianity has been around, believers didn't have the privilege of holding God's Word bound in beautiful leather. The printing press wasn't even invented until 1405, which means that for more than thirteen centuries, the early church didn't have what we have in much of our modern world—the privilege of opening a personal Bible on a daily basis. But they did have the privilege of listening, seeing, feeling, learning from, and experiencing an ever-present Holy Spirit.

The apostle Paul, who gave us the majority of the New Testament, was led by the Spirit into an Arabic country for three years, being taught directly by God about the enormity of grace, the church as the bride, the Holy Spirit, and the fullness of salvation (Galatians 1:17–18). Can you imagine how our modern-day church leaders would react if a man who murdered scores of Christians got radically saved and moved to Arabia without a Bible or computer, only to emerge claiming that Jesus had been his teacher and that the Holy Spirit had commissioned him to be an apostle to equip the body of Christ?

Sometimes in our current church culture, it seems as if teaching a person to learn how to communicate with God as a real, relational Counselor and Helper has slipped into the "kooky" category of Christianity. The mind is praised, logic and study are exalted, and experiencing God outside of a corporate worship service or Bible reading can sometimes be looked down on—along with the tambourine players and flag wavers.

But if learning about the Bible with your logic, memorizing Scripture with your mind, worshiping for twenty-five minutes on a Sunday, and simply listening to fifty-two sermons a year actually changed our broken hearts, don't you think the body of Christ would look a bit different from the bleeding mess we've become? There's a reason the world doesn't want our Jesus, and it's because they don't want to look like us. We're addicted, depressed, jealous, divisive with betrayal and accusation just like they are—and we shoot at our own wounded, especially if they make us look bad. When we walk into services week after week to simply file new information about God into our brains, our heads get big and our hearts stay small—and sometimes very broken. But when we move from head knowledge into heart encounter, love changes everything from the inside out.

CULTIVATING INTIMACY WITH GOD

When I started having powerful, intimate, real encounters with Jesus, I didn't wake up one day and BAM!—God hijacked my heart to a diamond cave, where we started hanging out every day. That started occurring because I got purposeful with my heart healing.

During my third trimester of pregnancy with my baby girl, Luca Gold, I would get up to use the facilities several times a night, only to head back to bed and lay awake in a torturous limbo state of exhaustion. But instead of staring into the darkness annoyed, or turning on a boring movie to try to coax myself back to sleep, I started intentionally dialing my heart into prayerful connection with God, asking Jesus to meet me in our secret place: my diamond cave.

At first, it was a bit difficult. I would close my eyes and take a deep breath, attempting to silence the thoughts that trolled through my brain to keep my mind racing in the late-night hours. My head always seemed to be bombarded with lists of things I needed to get done the next day. Because a head filled with important lists is hard to turn off, many times I would roll over to my journal and quickly write down everything I needed to accomplish—emptying my worried brain on paper so my heart could rest.

If I still found it hard to engage, then I would try listening to music. Because I wanted to see and hear Jesus with an imagination wide open, I would pop in my earbuds and choose an album without lyrics, sinking deeply into each note.

I would also have all sorts of descriptive Scriptures ready to go, like the one in Psalm 16:8–9 (TPT), where we're told: *"For I experience your wrap-around presence every moment. My heart and soul explode with joy—full of glory! Even my body will rest confident and secure."* I would imagine the arms of Father around my body, my heart exploding with joy and glory as I saw what Scripture clearly describes as reality. *"And His fullness fills you,"* Ephesians 2:1 (TPT) tells us, so I would watch as every cell of my body filled up with the overflowing light of God. *"He raised us up with Christ the exalted One, and we ascended with him into the glorious perfection and authority of the heavenly realm,"* so I would see my spirit flying up above all my worldly problems and sitting down in the throne room—*"for we are now joined as one with Christ!"* (Ephesians 2:6 TPT).

This passage in Ephesians became one of my favorites, and I would imagine myself opening the door to Jesus' heart and crawling inside, getting all nice and cozy, safe from harm while surrounded by perfect love. Before my mind was conscious of what had happened, envisioning the vivid descriptions of Scripture had opened the eyes of my heart to see Jesus. My spirit, soul, and body were actually *encountering* Him.

Every night for more than two months, I would cycle through the same routine, ending up in my secret diamond cave to hang out with a man who was so in love with me, my physical body felt as if it might eventually burst. At first, it would take time to experience Jesus' voice and His presence, but the more consistently I engaged and pressed in, the easier it was to feel His embrace.

When we first started meeting in the night watches, I expected us to do all sorts of spiritual things—like interceding for the nations or plumbing the deep mysteries of God. But most times, He just wanted to be with me, and I would end up lying against His chest and looking up at the diamonds that sparkled above us in protection, listening to His heart that beat for me. One time, I told Him how I would like to someday have a diamond necklace that I could wear as a physical representation of our secret place, quickly pushing the desire aside for more practical dreams. But Jesus just smiled at the request, as if scheming behind the scenes.

Sometimes He would tell me jokes, and I'd shake my bed with muffled chuckles—hoping not to wake up Luke as he slept beside me. One time, Jesus sat down on the white, fluffy bed He had built into the floor of our diamond cave, wanting to play patty-cake together. And though I thought it was rather silly at first, we ended up being so uncoordinated with our claps, we both eventually rolled on our sides bursting with laughter, having more fun than I'd had in a long time.

I finally got up the nerve to ask Him why He just wanted to hang out (which seemed like a waste of time in a world filled with such need), instead of doing purposeful things like praying for people or letting Him teach me. And His response was more than startling.

"Christa," He said kindly, "the only way you've ever known how to relate to Me is by doing something for Me—serving, worshiping, studying, and praying. But that's not why I created you. I created you to have an intimate friendship—and this is intimacy, sweet girl. If we're going to go forward and deepen our relationship, moving you from a servant to a friend, I want you to learn how to just be with Me—because I love your company more than anything in the universe. Once we establish that kind of relationship and you know My heart the way I know yours, believe Me—you will start living from your heart, a heart made whole."

It takes more intentionality to learn how to commune with a God who is real—seeking to know His voice, His personality, and His heart—than it does to pick up a book and dutifully learn about Him. When you approach God—who just happens to be the most important, intimate, loving, compassionate, powerfully *real* relationship you'll ever have—it seems kind of silly to just devote yourself to a life-time of books to learn about Him with your intellect when He's made a way for you to *experience* Him with all of your heart. It seems ridiculous to serve Him tirelessly with your earthly hands *more than* actually hearing, feeling, touching, and knowing the One you are serving.

Cultivating an intimate relationship with God doesn't mean sitting in a monastery for the rest of your life in meditation. Rather, it's learning to bring God into every part of your existence, including your finances, conversations, relationships, schoolwork, time, cooking, eating, sleeping, and drinking. Before David was ever crowned king, he included God in his everyday life, spending hours in a field where he tended his sheep. And every day, as he wrote love songs, listened, communed, and let God train his hands and give him strategies to overcome lions and bears, David became a man after God's own heart—because his heart learned to remain in constant connection.

If you've had traumatic experiences with rejection that have defined your life, then you need to have a *greater* experience with the God of acceptance to redefine your heart. If you've had experiences with trauma, then you need to have *greater* experiences with the Healer to bind up your wounds. If you've had experiences with lack, then you need to have *greater* encounters with God's abundance to rewire your beliefs.

It's easier than you think—especially when the person you're seeking to encounter is living inside of you. You simply have to choose to dial your heart into the Presence that's been waiting for you. David wrote:

"Where could I go from your Spirit?
Where could I run and hide from your face?
If I go up to heaven, you're there!
If I go down to the realm of the dead, you're there too!
If I fly with wings into the shining dawn, you're there!

If I fly into the radiant sunset, you're there waiting!
Wherever I go, your hand will guide me;
your strength will empower me.
It's impossible to disappear from you
or to ask the darkness to hide me;
for your presence is everywhere bringing light into
my night!" *(Psalm 139:7–11 TPT)*

Cultivating intimacy with God is learning to live uncovered before Love—the love that sees everything and never pushes you away. It's coming to understand that all barriers, coverings, blockages, and walls have been permanently removed by the blood of Jesus. It's finding out how to spend each moment with your heart tuned into the person who made His permanent home inside—beginning to listen, rest, laugh, commune, chat, and work as friends, comrades, lovers, and partners in this life.

Take a moment to bask in this heavenly truth—that you're already living in the light of unconditional love, forever graced with the intimate affection you were created for. You are, and forever will be, one with perfect Love.

Open-Heart Surgery

1. Are there places in your life that you're petrified of anyone seeing? What are the things about your life that you're most ashamed of, and what parts of you do you believe are unlovable?

2. Although the reality is that nothing can separate you from Father's love, you can turn away and refuse to receive that love out of shame. Have you struggled to believe that God only loves you *if*? At the core of your heart, do you believe you can only be loved if you're better, more obedient, less sinful, or less shameful?

3. Take several minutes, close your eyes, and meditate on your *oneness* with the Trinity. Your sins have been erased, leaving you eternally connected with Jesus. See yourself intertwined with that love, giving it access to every part of you—even the parts of you that need to change— knowing that you are loved anyway.

4. Do you experience your relationship with God in your head, or in your heart? If you know more *about* God than actually *know* God, then take a moment in confession, asking Him to reveal His true nature to your heart. It's time to live a lifestyle of communion with a very real, very powerful God. Go somewhere quiet and close your eyes, asking the Holy Spirit to make Himself known. If you need music, then turn on music. If you need Scriptures ready to go, then read them to encounter the *Living Word,* and see each Scripture with the eyes of your heart. Make time each day to experience God with all your heart, maybe every time you go get a snack in the kitchen, when you get in your car alone, or when you lay your head on your pillow. What is Father saying to your heart today?

Chapter 8

Your Heart-Brain Connection

When I was pregnant with my son Moses, Luke and I headed into a routine ultrasound at 36 weeks to check his progress. As the technician ran her tool over my belly to make the measurements, her brow furrowed with an obvious look of concern. Moses's brain was measuring at only 30 weeks and his body at 29 weeks, hard evidence that there might be something wrong with my umbilical cord's ability to get my son the nourishment he needed to develop normally.

It was a gloomy Valentine's Day when I pulled the passenger door closed outside the doctor's office, trying to stay dry from the rain that matched the storm raging in my heart, flooding my brain with overwhelming fear for my unborn son. I tried, very unsuccessfully, to swat the fearful thoughts away from my mind, but the medical report filled my head with tormenting worst-case scenarios.

"Okay, Father," I said, my eyes closed in prayer, "I know what the doctors say is *true*; Moses is in trouble. But my heart needs to know the *truth* about what *you* say about my son."

In an almost audible voice that shook my body with a

thunderous roar, the Spirit of God released His view of the situation into my heart with the concrete words, *"He is fine."* In an instant, peace, faith, and rest gushed out of my heart to relax my brain and my physical body with the tangible presence of the King.

I turned with wide eyes to Luke as he started up the car, reassured by the certainty of heaven's promise.

"Babe," I said calmly, "Moses is fine. My head doesn't just know it, *but my heart believes it."*

Sometimes when we get a bad report, our brains and bodies run frantically to get the prayer chains going through email and Facebook, calling our churches and friends to pray while our worried hearts ignore the Counselor, Helper, and Comforter who lives inside. But the Holy Spirit is always ready and willing to show us God's view of the situation. When we run to our Bible promises and begin declaring them logically with our brains, at times we don't allow the Living Word—Jesus—to emerge from the center of hearts where we hold our core beliefs.

There's no faith involved in quick, frantic approaches to difficult situations, because faith comes from hearing, and hearing through the Word of God (Romans 10:17). And hearing is *relational*. If the Living Word is a person named Jesus who forever connected us to the Father and released the Spirit of Truth to live within our hearts, then it makes much more sense to stop, wait, and listen to Him before we listen to fear. Prayer isn't about throwing Scriptures and pleas up towards heaven in hopes that one of them might work and pan out on earth. Rather, prayer is about living at the feet of Jesus in intimate relationship, then listening to everything

He has to say about our current situation. Once we have a word from Him through the counseling Holy Spirit, we need only come into agreement with what He's already praying.

My responsibility that difficult Valentine's Day wasn't to throw out anxious prayers to a faraway heaven, or to try to muster up pretend faith that I didn't have. My responsibility was to stay connected to an actual person alive within me, and then experience His truth within my heart. When I did just that, God poured in real faith like an overflowing waterfall.

Two days after we had received our gloomy medical report, a peaceful girl and her confident husband walked into an ultrasound room again, in complete trust from the word of truth that God had released into our hearts. As the medical technician's face turned from worried to clearly confused, she looked over at me and Luke to confirm God's miracle.

"Well, I'm not sure what happened to this baby within two days," she said, sitting back in her chair in surprise. "But your son is measuring at thirty-six weeks all around. And *he is fine.*"

At that point on my heart-healing journey, I hadn't had my diamond cave experience, and parts of the hard drive of my heart were definitely still damaged, divided, and in pain. These parts were still filled with programs that continued to run with fear, hurt, and distrust towards God on a daily basis. But in that particular situation, I chose to bypass those wounds and head directly to the source—a real person who wanted me to experience the peace that only He can give.

If I hadn't stopped to encounter God, asking Him what He thought about my unborn son, I can guarantee that medical report would have crashed through the gateway of my brain, running into my heart like a toxic computer virus to short my circuits with anxiety. But because I chose to let God minister to my heart *first*, His truth and love filled me with such faith that I began to pray in accordance with what He was revealing deep within. The intermittent thoughts of fear that came over the course of those two days were easy to kick out of my head before they became permanent problems within my heart.

THE "WHAT-IFS?"

One of my spiritual fathers lives so intimately with Jesus, he hasn't moved from the peace of that relationship into fear or frustration in more than seventeen years, even when the storms of life roll in. He's learned to live like Jesus, the ultimate storm sleeper, who had so much peace on the inside that He was able to command the winds and waves to cease, bringing peace on the outside. I, however, am not quite at that level, even though that is the goal. At times, my imagination still slips through my consciousness, taking me to scary places in my head that never should be visited.

With a writing deadline quickly approaching, I am bunkering down to write in a sprint for a few days while my husband and son are visiting my in-laws so I can work undistracted. As I was getting ready for bed last night, and our old 1899 Victorian house began its usual creaking and popping, I had a random, fearful thought that was quite unusual for me. *What if someone breaks in tonight while I'm sleeping, and I'm all alone?* Before I was even conscious of my actions, I had put chairs in front of several doors, locking myself into my bedroom (which I never did before), and hidden a weapon by the bed within arm's reach. My usually peaceful imagination went on a wild ride—seeing armed, masked men breaking in to rob me as I planned out all the things I would say to anyone who dared invade my home.

As I lay in bed and turned off the light, immersed in my fictional imagined scenario, my heart was racing, blood boiling, fear writhing, and eyes tearing. The power of my imagination had taken a fake scenario and made it as real as if it was actually happening, filling my heart with all sorts of negative emotions that were clearly influencing my chemical and physical makeup.

Dr. Amit Sood, a professor of medicine at the Mayo Clinic, tells us that within our brains, the imaginary is real, lighting up the same nerve bundles whether the event is actually happening, or just imagined. We use our imaginations every day. Children use this gift to make a few chairs and a blanket turn into a castle, or a towel tied over their shoulders into a Superman cape. Some people use this gift to envision lustful scenarios for sexual pleasure, or worst-case situations like natural disasters, financial difficulties, and relational explosions. The majority of the "what-if" scenarios that we allow to roll through our brains never come close to happening, but these imagined scenes are so powerful, they end up dictating our responses and actions and ruining our present moments with unnecessary emotions.

If all of us are already using our imaginations every day, many times to envision negative things, shouldn't we learn how to use them in a sanctified way to draw close to Jesus?

OPENING THE EYES OF YOUR HEART

Paul wrote to the Ephesians, "I pray that the eyes of your heart may be enlightened in order that you may know the hope to which he has called you" (Ephesians 1:18 NIV). But when you ask people to turn on *all of their heart* to experience God, some get very nervous that you're asking them to turn off their brain. And that would just be silly, wouldn't it? In fact, the condition of your heart is most affected by the three-pound organ sitting inside your skull. Your brain is critical in your heart-healing because, according to Hebrew Scripture, it is the gatekeeper of your heart, determining what will come in and out.

Let's put it into computer terms. Your brain is the processor of all your thinking, and your heart is the hard drive of the whole operation. Neither of them can work without the other one being involved. If your heart is healed and whole, centered in love and intimacy with God, then the computer of your heart will naturally send out good information through the gateway of your brain, and your thoughts will be filled with life and love.

But what if you watch the news and find out that a murderer is on the loose in your neighborhood? Your mind gets uploaded with a file that has a computer virus of fear attached to it. If your heart is wounded with fear from the past, then the gateway of your mind will allow the new information about the murder to swirl like a tornado, doing more damage inside. But if the eyes of your heart are open and you are locked into relationship with God, you can immediately run to the counsel of the Holy Spirit and get a direct word about the situation. Your relationship will actually guard your mind with peace and keep the gateway of the brain closed, blocking that virus from downloading fear into the heart's mainframe. "Then you will *experience God's peace*, which exceeds anything we can understand," writes Paul. "*His peace will guard your hearts and minds* as you live in Christ Jesus" (Philippians 4:7 NLT, italics mine).

It always surprises me when people get nervous about using the eyes of their heart to encounter God—especially since Scripture is loaded with examples of this. The Mosaic law warned only against making or worshiping *physical* images of God, but one glance through the Psalms proves that the Hebrew culture loved to imagine God in all sorts of ways to engage with their beloved Creator.

> "You're as real to me as bedrock beneath my feet,
> like a castle on a cliff, my forever firm Fortress,
> my Mountain of hiding, my Pathway of escape,
> my Tower of rescue where none can reach me.
> My secret Strength and Shield around me,
> you are Salvation's Ray of Brightness shining on
> the hillside." *(Psalm 18:2 TPT)*

> "The LORD is my Shepherd, . . .
> You prepare a table before me . . . .
> You anoint my head with oil."
>
> *(Psalm 23:1, 5 NIV)*

"Here's the one thing I crave from God . . . :
I want the privilege of living with him every moment in
  his house,
finding the sweet loveliness of his face."
(Psalm 27:4 TPT)

"His massive arms are wrapped around you, protecting
  you.
You can run under his covering of majesty and hide.
His arms of faithfulness are a shield keeping you from
  harm."
(Psalm 91:4 TPT)

"My sobs came right into your heart
and you turned your face to rescue me."
(Psalm 18:6 TPT)

I use the imagination God gave me every time I read Scripture, looking through the eyes of my heart. I will sit in a coffee shop imagining Jesus across from me, opening my phone so people don't think I'm crazy when I chat out loud with Him about all sorts of things in Scripture. I love opening up the Bible to read the parables that Jesus taught, seeing the father running fast towards his prodigal son, covering his filth and shame with a beautiful robe. In fact, whenever I start to feel shame in any way and need a good dose of the reality of forgiveness, I close my eyes and imagine this story with me as the prodigal, seeing Father running towards me in my pain, not away from me, and then loving me so much that He takes off His robe and covers my dirty rags. Every time my heart *sees* the truth of this good Father within my heart, it gets easier and easier to actually *experience* His grace.

I love meditating and thinking about things that are lovely, pure, true, just, honorable, and commendable, as Philippians 4:8 tells us to do. I love to remember the Lord's death when I take Communion, closing my eyes in prayer to see His bleeding frame on the cross, overwhelmed with gratitude and love for my Savior (1 Corinthians 11:26). Revelation 4 is one of my favorite chapters, depicting the actual throne room of the living God, where Ephesians 2:6 tells us we're already seated with Christ. I love to "fix my eyes on Jesus" by reading descriptions of Him on the earth and in heaven, then asking the Holy Spirit to help me see Him as He truly is, not how I have perceived Him to be (Hebrews 12:2).

For years I had focused on all my problems, trying to change myself through study, works, and dutiful service. But concentrating on my problems always left me feeling ashamed, and focusing on all my negatives only seemed to produce more negatives. Yet, seeing Jesus kept making me more like Jesus. Each night as I spent more intentional time talking, laughing, resting, and just hanging out with Him, I found that my heart started recognizing His abiding presence during the daylight hours. In fact, it was as if the overflow of our time together was spilling into everything, and as a result, my thoughts, emotions, speech, and actions were changing—to the point where my husband and family started to notice.

The more I communed with the solution *first*—the presence of the living God—the more His goodness, kindness, and love began to fill up the rooms in my heart and kick out old, unwanted tenants of fear, shame, bitterness, and anger. It was like I was being stretched and pulled outward and upward, creating more and more capacity inside for abundant life to keep bursting out.

EXPANDING YOUR HEART'S CAPACITY

When Moses came into our world, we couldn't keep our eyes, hands, and lips off him, smothering our new little bundle with endless kisses and cuddles. As his big, blue eyes began to develop and focus, every day I would pick up my newborn son and face him upwards on my lap—his eyes locked with mine as we smiled and giggled at one another, forming our bond with joyful connection. I started to notice that almost every time we went through our routine, Moses would eventually roll his eyes and look away, as if he was transfixed on a spaceship in the sky, checking out with a blank stare.

All babies have to develop the capacity to experience healthy bonding, and this process is especially important between the ages of six and twelve months. When babies see the smiling face of someone who is genuinely happy to be with them, the brain computes the message in a sixth of a second—before they have time to be conscious of it. And according to most experts, babies rely primarily on a strong bond with their mothers in the first two years for their brains to develop. A mother actually synchronizes her brain with her baby through left eye to left eye contact, bouncing her emotional signal back and forth continuously. Whatever emotion you feel for your baby is chemically reproduced and imprinted within their brain, helping them to develop their own self-image. You can never hide your right brain emotion from your baby's right brain, trying to fake a signal. Baby's right brain can always detect how you really feel from the left side of your face.

No wonder Scripture tells us over and over to seek the face of God. If looking into your mother's face helped build neural pathways in your brain to match her emotions, then think about what happens every time you're in the presence of Jesus, looking into His face. The more you're in communion with the Trinity who loves you unconditionally, the more that love is imprinted onto your heart and mind. But if your capacity to receive that love is limited, then your attachment to Jesus can feel tenuous.

Capacity refers to the maximum amount that something can contain. When a baby looks into the face of someone who is glad to be with them, the strengthening bond delights it and its joy tank quickly reaches its capacity. The infant's brain is still developing, building greater capacity as the neurons are forming pathways over time. So initially, an infant has very few pathways able to handle the emotions of joy and delight, which causes it to look away when their tank gets filled up and their circuits are overloaded.

Dr. Jim Wilder, esteemed neurotheologian and one of the authors of the book *The Life Model: Living from the Heart Jesus Gave You*, describes this like being tickled too much. When you can't stand it anymore, you feel like you're going to explode. A little baby who has reached their capacity for joy will break eye contact and look away, and a responsive parent will match their emotion, waiting for their child to look back and connect once again. Every time this cycle happens, Dr. Wilder calls it *Climbing Joy Mountain*, where the baby's brain exceeds capacity for joy, stimulating more nerve development in the brain. As this beautiful transference of joy exchanges between parent and child on a regular basis, the baby becomes able to develop a secure attachment, both emotionally and physiologically.

For many years my heart was a building filled up with a mixture of life and pain—but the pain took up a good chunk of my inner real estate and held a lot of the voting power. I had reached my capacity, and I couldn't hold anything else. As a result, I had a very small section able to cope with new challenges when they came my way. I discovered that every time I encountered a trial—big or small—I would quickly reach my limit to handle the problem and either explode in frustrated anger, run to numb myself, check out completely, or sprint away in retreat.

Your heart has a limited amount of real estate space, too, and if that space is filled to capacity with your own unhealed hurts, believe me—you're not going to have much capacity for dealing with new pain when it comes along, much less the pain of others. In fact, you will only be able to deal with others' pain to the extent that you have dealt with your own. The greater your capacity, the more you can deal with. Conversely, if the challenge in front of you is greater than the capacity you have to deal with it, you end up reacting in ways you wish you hadn't.

ink of *capacity* and *challenge* set on opposite sides of scale. When you go through a big challenge, it puts a ton of bricks on one side of your scale—weighing you down with pain. Those bricks could be anything from losing a loved one or getting stabbed in the back, to finding yourself fired and hitting financial disaster. To rebalance your inner scale, you need to have a heavy amount of heart-capacity on the other side to deal with the challenge; otherwise, those bricks of tragedy will take you down, leaving you unable to cope.

When challenge is greater than capacity, you can get stuck in the pain instead of being able to walk through it to the other side. But as you live to keep your heart connected with Jesus, building space inside for constant relationship, the good side of your scale gets weighty with gold bars of love, joy, hope, trust, and peace. As challenges continue to arise, you're now grounded with internal resources to handle problems without tipping your scales towards negative emotions. As you build heart-capacity with Jesus, He equips you with inner solutions to thrive in every challenge.

The thing is, many people are so filled up with unhealed hurts, the only capacity they have left to deal with new challenges is about the size and weight of a penny. If you lay a penny on your capacity scale, it only takes a tiny rock on the other side—like bad traffic, running late, or someone looking at you funny—to pull you down and leave you unable to cope. This is why building your heart capacity with Jesus and letting Him take more real estate inside is the most important thing you can do while breathing on the planet. As my favorite speaker, Graham Cooke, says, "If the enemy can't penetrate your peace, he doesn't know what to do with you."

When we teach our hearts to live in unity with the Love

that's always available—inside a life-giving relationship that fills us with truth, joy, peace, and intimate encounters with a real being—our heart expands and our brain works *for* us instead of *against* us. The thoughts and pictures that come out of our brains actually begin to strengthen connection instead of weaken it. They even shape our physical and chemical makeup.

YOUR BRAIN WAS MADE FOR LOVE

I'm about as close to being a scientist as I am the tooth fairy, but over the years on my personal road to heart-healing, I have learned a thing or two about how both body and heart are influenced by the brain.

When you came out of the womb, you were already a physical, emotional, and spiritual being. Yet, none of your three parts came out fully developed. Instead, each part continued to grow and change as you experienced life. Baby brain science proves that each fetus—no matter what culture, race, or gender—undergoes critical brain development inside the womb and newborn stages of life that affect all sorts of physical and emotional outcomes.

In the same way nutrition determines how a baby's body develops physically, love and affection determine how the child develops emotionally. A baby's body will stop growing and become sick if there's a shortage of food or nutrition, and a baby's brain development will suffer if there has been a lack of positive emotional stimulation for the heart. Fortunately, God created everything about us to be redeemable and renewable—especially in the realm of our hearts and minds. *We aren't stuck with the brain we were born with.* Our brain is *neuroplastic* (*neuro* means brain, *plastic* means able to change), which proves that our thought life can actually change the physical and chemical structure of our brain. This is important to understand, because *everything that was lost can be restored.*

Out of all the physical brains on the planet, God created the human brain to be far superior to the rest. All brains begin with a basic reptilian model, formed around a brain stem for simple life functions of survival, but yours added and expanded as time went on, learning traits such as nurture and care like other mammals. But what really sets your human brain apart on planet earth is how it continued to develop outer layers as life began to unfold. This special part of your brain is called the cerebral cortex.

When you were just a little baby, the first year of your life was all about making brain connections, and your brain was born with billions of cells called neurons that needed to be linked up through your experiences. As life happened around you, these neurons connected themselves into trillions of neural pathways called synapses, which outnumber the stars in the entire universe. But if your nerve cells (neurons) didn't make the connections, the cells died. That's why the most powerful way for your brain to make connections in infancy was through quality parent-child attachment.

There has been some debate in recent years about the roles of the right and left hemispheres of the brain, a debate that I'm definitely not qualified to chime in on. But generally speaking, all scientists agree that the brain works best when both sides—right and left—are healthy and synchronized with one another.

Sitting on the top right side of your brain is your right prefrontal cortex. This part of the brain is the source of all emotions, and it doesn't know by being told—it knows by *experience*. Your right brain is visual and nonverbal and takes in the whole picture at once. It understands what someone is trying to say by their tone of voice, not by the words coming out of their mouth. In fact, the right brain doesn't hear words, but instead computes melodies, intonation, pictures, and rhythms. Your right brain *feels* before it *understands*. And as it fires up inside, it's much faster than the conscious thought of the left hemisphere.

This past year while I was speaking at a conference in New York City, Luke got Moses dressed up in head-to-toe dinosaur gear to take him to the Natural History Museum. As my three-year-old son walked the halls of that enormous building, his right brain learned just how big dinosaurs were when he stood in front of their enormous skeletons, completely freaking out in the best way possible. Moses firmly and accurately believed that T. rexes were gigantic because he had *experienced* them as he stared up in awe at an actual thirteen-foot frame.

After that encounter, the information about the enormity of a T. rex was sent over and stored in Moses's left prefrontal cortex, filing it away as fact. You, too, use the filing cabinet of your left brain to store up autobiographical memories. The left brain is what allows you to speak your language and decipher the words of others. God created our left brains to name and explain things—using logic, analysis, and reasoning skills. It's the seat of all language and words, factual stories and descriptions.

And believe me, your left brain does not want to change its beliefs once they have been formed and filed away.

If Moses had come back to our hotel room from his adventure and I had tried to convince his left brain with words and logic that I could fit a T. rex in my pocket, he never would have believed me. No matter what I would have said, Moses's right brain had *experienced* how big dinosaurs are, then filed that information as fact in his left brain. His left brain wasn't going to change its mind just because Mommy said something different. In order for Moses to ever believe that T. rexes were tiny, he would need to see and encounter a pocket-sized T. rex to rewire his left brain.

Did you catch that? When you experience something, your brain believes and files it away as fact. Which is why, when you experience God, it sure gets easy to believe Him, forming concrete facts about His goodness.

From what I've seen over years as a believer, a lot of our ministry techniques in the church are aimed at our left brain, and we're beating our head with our Bibles trying to make it believe that God is good in a world where we experience a whole lot of bad. I have been in church after church where people file in, sing a few songs where they pour out their hearts, hear a factual sermon with their left brain, and leave again—never encountering the God they came to learn about. When we try to logically convince ourselves to believe scriptural precepts without learning to experience the Author, it's about the same thing as if I try to convince Moses that all T. rexes are pocket-sized. It's just not going to happen—especially when every heart on this earth has *experienced* deep amounts of tragedy—and God seemed absent, silent, distant, or unfaithful.

I know I'm hammering this principle home, but if you've experienced life to be unsafe, then you need a *greater* experience with the God who is Protector. If you've encountered a life of rejection, then you need a *greater* encounter with the God who is Unconditional Love. If you've known sickness, then you need a *greater* reality with the Healer who came to bind up our wounds. As a believer, you must move from head knowledge about God to an intimate heart-relationship with Him—one in which you're *experiencing* His presence, voice, and touch upon your life moment by moment.

You were created to live a lifestyle of *encounter.*

I lived my whole life *knowing* the head knowledge that Jesus loved me, but never *believing* it until I *encountered* His love on a regular basis within our fellowship together. I knew logically that the Spirit of the Lord brings freedom, but I didn't believe it enough to live free—not until I had encountered the God who healed my pain and set me free. For many years, I stored up Scripture in my head and declared it in religious discipline, trying to change my mind and convince my brain to believe.

But my right brain had *experienced* abuse and filed it away in my left brain as fact. My right brain had *encountered* physical sickness that went unhealed, locking in my beliefs. My right brain had *known* so much rejection that my left brain had a huge case against God's love. If my mind was ever going to change and believe the truth, my heart needed to have an encounter with the truth. I needed to know that

Jesus is closer than my pain. I needed to know Love greater than all my fear.

Trust is birthed in a safe relationship, and that relationship is available to you. If you ever want to convince yourself of the truth, all you have to do is encounter the Living Truth. A genius God decided to make His home inside you, and when your heart begins to encounter a very real, very present Redeemer in relationship—One who promises to transform and restore you from within—the healing that takes place will naturally produce redeemed thoughts. Your brain cells will then start firing and creating new connections, reshaping the physical structure. Every part of your brain that might be in a deficit because of your past can be repaired and restored by being in relationship with someone who wants to be with you.

Jesus wants a relationship with you so badly that He suffered and died to make this a constant reality. This means that just because your mother was depressed, abusive, or neglectful in your childhood, imprinting her brain chemistry onto yours, it doesn't mean your brain has to stay that way as an adult—especially when your heavenly parents, the Father, Son, and Holy Spirit, get ahold of you. Just because you were raised without the nurture and affection you needed to build healthy attachments in childhood doesn't mean you cannot attach to Christ. In fact, He took the first step by attaching Himself to you permanently through salvation, securing your oneness (Colossians 1:21–22)! The more you allow the Word and Spirit to penetrate deep, leading you into a supernatural encounter with a real God who manifests His presence within you, the more His nurture and affection will heal your heart, change your thinking, and physically restore all that was lost.

Your body is linked to your brain, and your brain is linked to your heart. As your heart becomes the primary focus of your life and you learn how to keep it connected and tuned into intimacy, your mind naturally changes. Your brain actually rewires, and your physical composition manifests the healing power of *sozo*—the fullness of salvation.

Open-Heart Surgery

1. Do you ever wait to hear what Father is saying before you pray, developing a relationship that is truly intimate? Take a few moments and sit at the feet of Jesus, asking Him about a certain situation in your life that needs a miracle. Does a Scripture come to mind? Do you hear a still, small voice? Did a song come on the radio, or a fleeting thought stroll through your mind? God is always speaking to you. Sit at His feet today and dial your heart into His voice.

2. Scientifically speaking, what is imagined is real. So what are you using your imagination for each day? Do you struggle with speculations, or maybe taking trips into the future to think about all sorts of "what-ifs"? How could you use your imagination to encounter God instead?

3. Meditating on the Word of God to encounter His presence is one of the most powerful things you can do to build intimacy. Using the descriptive Scriptures on pages 163–64 or finding some visual Scriptures of your own,

read each word with eyes closed and ask God to help you *see* what you're reading.

4. After learning about capacity versus challenge, how would you describe the capacity in your heart? Are you filled to capacity with old wounds, making it easy for you to blow a fuse from very small challenges, or are you filled to capacity with peace, giving you grace to deal with difficult circumstances when they arise?

5. Take a moment and think about your brain and its neuroplasticity. If you are not stuck with the brain you were born with, then are you willing to start rewiring your brain for love and connection? If so, take several minutes, opening the eyes of your heart with the Holy Spirit to *see* the face of Jesus. Look into His eyes. What do they look like? What are they filled with? How does He see you? As you gaze into the eyes of truth, your brain will rewire with the perspective of heaven.

Chapter 9

A Heart Made Whole

On February 13, 2014, Luke and I made a last-minute decision to throw an overnight bag together, fasten Moses into his car seat, and head east on I-20 for a three-hour road trip. Some of our best friends were renewing their wedding vows the next day on the perfect day for love to be celebrated, Valentine's Day, and we wanted to stand with them in support.

Moses and I woke up February 14, along with my friend Katie and her four daughters, to roses, petals, and gifts laid out all over their house in our honor. Each rose had been removed of thorns late into the night by her sweet husband so as not to prick their young girls. Handwritten letters from our thoughtful men expressed their deepest affection—and chocolates showed how well they knew us.

After a perfect morning filled with hugs, kisses, and a bit of a sugar rush, Katie and I went out running errands after breakfast—my eight-months-pregnant belly and evident waddle announcing that Luca Gold would be arriving within the month. The boys had headed out again with more Valentine's Day schemes, and we all met back up again around lunchtime. Katie's husband, John, sat us both down on a couch, holding two white bags with blue ribbon in his hands. But instead of looking at her, he looked at me first.

"Christa," he said, while smiling over at Luke, "this morning when I was praying in the shower, I heard very clearly that I needed to go get something for you today."

"Me?"

I put my hand to my chest and glanced over at Katie, who burst out in laughter. My friend's eyes were sparkling in playful jest.

"Should I be worried?" she giggled, knowing that if her husband had heard something from God, he was more than encouraged by her to listen and obey.

"Well, keep going," she said to John. "Go ahead and give it to her, because I see from the second bag, you got something for me, too!"

As John laid a beautiful white bag on my lap and backed away, I felt nervous to untie the thick blue ribbon and look inside. The packaging alone was unlike any gift I'd ever been given, and I knew this wasn't just any sort of present; this was a gift of great worth.

As I pulled out a dark maroon jewelry box, my heart raced while tracing along the opening. I drew the lid upward to reveal the contents inside, and I gasped in shock.

You see, John didn't know about the secret place where I had been hanging out with Jesus each night, and not even my husband was aware of what my heart had whispered in desire. But on instruction from heaven, John had gone out to buy me a specific gift.

Inside that perfect little box was a necklace formed into a circle of black diamonds with white diamonds filling the center. The very thing I had asked Jesus for—my diamond cave necklace.

ONE THING REMAINS

The kindness of God overwhelms my heart every time I think about that story. Though I believe beyond a shadow of a doubt that God never willed and orchestrated Goldie's disease, He still knew that death would come knocking at my door just weeks later on March 5. My beautiful Father had made sure that I had something tangible to hold onto—a specific reminder of who He is and who He wanted to be for me in that excruciating moment.

As Luke lay weeping on the floor, rocking the lifeless body of our daughter, I had reached up around my neck, grabbing hold of the new necklace and gripping it so tightly my knuckles drained white. In that moment I knew that if I chose to put Jesus on the other side of the black wall again, who knows if I'd ever invite Him close again. If I let my heart be poisoned with offense, I would be drinking the very death that would kill my own soul.

With the eyes of my heart fixed on heaven, I closed my eyes and saw my cave of diamonds covering the horrific scene unfolding in the bedroom. I could see the ceiling sparkling with brilliant light, glory streaming all around. I felt the warm arms of the Comforter begin to wrap around me. Yes, I had sustained horrific damage, and yes, most of my heart was unrecognizable. *But nothing was lost.* As the bomb of death threatened to destroy my heart, my ceiling of diamonds was a force so strong, it held every shattered piece within the blast zone of my diamond cave. Which also meant that every piece of my heart was still within arm's reach of my kind, strong, and precious Jesus. The new heart inside of me remained heavily anchored to His goodness, and more than ever within my agony, I was convinced that He was the only one who could put me back together.

As I lay in bed, I took a deep breath, knowing that I needed to intentionally lift my eyes away from death and find the eyes of my Savior, singing a song that would remind my heart of the truth. For fourteen years I had been a songwriter, crafting songs sung in churches far and wide. Yet, many times the final product was scripturally sound and melodically catchy, but not something I had personally lived out. In 2010, I wrote the words to a bridge that I had belted out too many times to count, never understanding the weight of my declaration. But here in my greatest pain, gripping my diamond necklace, I lifted my head to heaven, looked at Jesus, and sang to my Prince of Peace:

"In death, in life
I'm confident and covered by the power of your great love.
My debt is paid
There's nothing that can separate my heart
From your great love."

—"One Thing Remains,"
written by Brian Johnson, Christa Black
Gifford, and Jeremy Riddle

In the days and months that followed Goldie's death, the fire of death burned like hell, but I was never alone in the flames. When the moments of pain became too excruciating to bear, I would run into the sheltering arms of the Healer. I learned that there were no shortcuts to the grieving process and that brutal honesty was required. If I wanted my smashed heart to be put back together, I had to face and embrace *all* my emotions.

PERMISSION TO FEEL

Since I knew half the town, it seemed like half the town brought by meal after meal, flowers, toilet paper, and anything else they thought we might need immediately after our loss. The kindness that poured in from friends, churches, and strangers was overwhelming, and casseroles, platters, and homemade desserts piled up on my parents' kitchen counters, making it easy to take a bite every time I walked by.

One morning as I stood over the desserts, wanting to shove them all into my mouth to numb the pain in my heart, I burst into tears and ran to the bedroom where Goldie had lived and died, pulling the pink blankets still stained with her blood up close up to my face. It was the last trace of life on this earth still filled with her scent, and my arms ached with agonizing emptiness that wanted to hold on, breathe in deep, and never exhale.

Taking a moment to grab my bearings, I stopped, knowing that if I didn't receive comfort and release from the true source, I would be forced to run to a counterfeit affection. This pain was too heavy, too real, and too sharp. This pain begged like an addict for a fix, longing to escape reality simply to survive. But because I had been building my relationship with the Comforter—expanding my heart capacity with His presence—I was armed with firsthand experiences about how much better God was at His job than food, escapes, or substances ever had been.

I closed my eyes and tuned my heart towards heaven, thanking Jesus for sending me a Comforter for times like these, for my son Moses, my husband, my family, and all the blessings that had been pouring in as we navigated the unpredictable waters of grief. In an instant, the eyes of my heart could see my diamond cave covering me in protection and feel the presence of my sweet Jesus pulling me in close as I rested in His arms.

"Christa," He whispered softly to my spirit. "You have permission to feel every emotion right now. Don't suppress anything. Don't deny the truth inside your heart. Just feel, and then bring those feelings to me."

As I lay against the chest of my Savior, being granted permission to feel every emotion in my shattered heart, my physical body bent over in guttural wails and chokes. I reached so deeply inside the brokenness that at times the screams would fade to an eerie, open-mouthed silence that gushed with saliva and tears.

"I'm so angry, Jesus! I'm just so angry!" My face filled with red-hot blood that bubbled up from my soul with the intense fury of a mother forced to bury her only daughter. "I'm so mad that she's gone! That I'll never hold her again!

That I'll never hear the sound of her voice! It's not fair, Jesus, it's just not right!!" Moving in front of me to grab both of my arms, Jesus lifted my eyes to look straight into His.

"If you need something to punch, Christa, just punch me." His chest began to heave with sobs that matched my own. "Punch me, Christa—I can take it. Let me take it, friend. Let me have the full force of your anger."

With the strength of a thousand men in battle, fueled by the rage of death, I began to punch and punch and punch and punch—hitting Jesus in the chest, the arms, and the face. I screamed every time my fist made contact, unleashing the anger that threatened to poison my soul. I sobbed with every slap, pouring out the agony within.

When the last punch fell, so did I—collapsing into Jesus's arms again, soaking His garment with my tears. As I lay there weeping, I felt one of His arms wrap around my back while the other held my head close. I could hear His breathing shorten and heart rate increase. These weren't the breaths of a calm man at peace; they were the quick breaths of a man who wanted to rip someone to shreds.

I pulled back to look into His eyes, wondering why His countenance had changed. But instead of seeing the calm pools of sorrow and grief that I expected, tears filled with comforting empathy for my pain, I was staring into eyes that churned with rage. His face was burning red, His mouth closed and nostrils flaring, matching the rhythm of His quick, angry breaths. I saw the veins in His neck tighten, His brow furl, and His muscles tense up, fingers retracting to form tight fists that looked ready to punch through a wall.

With one hand, He reached over and rolled up His sleeve past His wrist, exposing deep scars that caved into a deep hole—the hole still visible from His crucifixion.

"Feel them, Christa," He said in a low voice, trying to get the words out as His voice shook. "Feel my scars."

I reached out my quivering fingers, placing them into the deep gashes that sank into His flesh, tears falling down my face in awe.

"Feel my side." He took my hand and quickly placed it over the side of His garment where I could feel the deep indentation of a hole replaced with scar tissue underneath my fingertips. My heart watched the face of my best friend fill with an anger far greater than my own. His fury rose up quickly, bursting out of every pore in His body, and He stared through me as if remembering a distant, painful memory.

"Who do you think could possibly possess more fury for your loss than Me—the One who bled so that she could live? Who could be more angry about Goldie's death than Me—the One who suffered and died so that it wouldn't have to happen!"

My mouth hung open, the weight of His words hitting me like an avalanche.

My Jesus had been crucified to conquer disease—the very disease that had taken the life of my daughter. My Jesus still bore the scars of death—the death that He died so that Goldie could live. My Jesus had walked the earth displaying the will of a good God to heal the sick, raise the dead, cleanse the lepers, and cast out evil—even telling us that we would do greater works than He did. And if my Jesus had been standing in front of me in the flesh, there is no doubt in my mind: my Goldie would have been instantly healed. But even though my Jesus had sealed the victory, this was a war in which tragic death and disease had still won on this earth.

We were both angry about it.

And that was completely okay.

Something foundational inside my heart healed that day when Jesus got angrier than I was about Goldie's death. I realized I had created such a distorted perception of Him over the years—picturing Him as a distant deity made of steel, void of feeling and emotion. But the real Jesus had loved me so much, He put on humanity with flesh and bone so He could relate to every emotion my heart could ever produce.

Jesus knew what my pain felt like firsthand, so He knew exactly what I needed when hurt tried to destroy my heart. Jesus knew the pain of betrayal from His dear friend and chosen companion, Judas. He knew the agony of watching His friend Mary weep at the loss of her brother Lazarus, then weeping with her—even though I believe He knew He was about to raise him back to life. My Savior knew how it felt to be falsely accused and not even defend Himself. He knew what it was like to be laughed at and scorned by His own. He knew violent rage for those who defiled His Father's temple as He fashioned a whip to drive out the money changers.

Jesus' intention for us as believers is never to suppress the truth of our emotions and put on fake religious smiles, attempting to deal with very natural feelings on our own. When life hurts, we hurt just as He did—and that's simply okay. He never wants us to beat up our hearts as they bleed, kicking our emotions to the side, quoting Scripture at them in anger, or willing ourselves to change. Pain brings deepest brokenness, and a hurting child always wants to run into the consoling, safe arms of a loving parent. Feeling our pain doesn't prove that we lack faith—it proves our need for constant connection with God.

In Scripture Jesus taught me how to express anguish because He sweat with drops of blood. He taught me how to weep, sob, and groan. He taught me how to be sad, to greatly desire, to be joyful, and then to overflow with compassion, peace, and love—facing each emotion while staying connected with the Father through the Holy Spirit. As I was given permission by Jesus to feel everything after Goldie's heart stopped beating—the good and the bad—I was also invited to remain in a friendship that bore the burden of my pain. Not for one second did I have to carry the emotions by myself, heal my own heart, or fix the mess. That was, and still is, Jesus' job. And He's really, really, really good at that. So much so that He showed me how to *thrive* inside the worst pain of my life.

THE POWER OF ACCEPTANCE

Over the course of the past year, when sorrow, grief, agony, hurt, and distress pounded down on my heart like acid rain, I discovered a secret of life that's changed everything. I discovered the power of *raw acceptance.*

Wholehearted living doesn't mean living void of pain. It means being so alive in every moment that we're also able to stay present without trying to escape—even when everything hurts like hell. But the only way to accomplish this is to learn to be with Someone inside of that pain—Someone so strong that He takes the pain and exchanges it for constant comfort, healing, counsel, hope, and love.

My favorite definition of joy is *someone is glad to be with me*. Because you're in Christ, you just happen to be forever connected to Someone who loves you so much, He died to remain connected no matter what. Happiness is circumstantial, and Jesus never expects us to be happy about the traumas that have broken our hearts. I will never be happy about burying my daughter, for good reasons. But joy is relational—and we never leave relationship with Him living inside. When we learn to keep our hearts open to the acceptance of two realities—trauma and relationship—we can experience the paradox of deepest sorrow and overflowing joy in the same breath, one never negating the other.

Each day as my heart would scream to be numbed, I would turn around and face the truth. And the truth is, I was in agony, not knowing how to survive the death of my daughter. I would close my eyes and see my bleeding heart—mangled, torn, and full of pain—knowing that without the right medicine, that pain could turn into diseases like bitterness, distrust, despair, and unforgiveness. So instead of ignoring my heart as it screamed, I would intentionally hand it over again and again to my best friend, Jesus.

In those moments of surrender, I learned the unfathomable power of raw acceptance and confession. "Jesus, this is where my heart is today, and it's a total mess," I would pray. "But I'm not going to condemn it for being a wreck, beat myself up, try to heal myself, or force myself to change. I'm going to accept that if this is where I am today—wounded and broken—then you will meet me right here in my pain and begin to heal me with your love." And then I would retreat to my secret diamond cave of intimacy and cry a bit more with Him.

For several months, we cried a lot together, and I never tried to stop the tears. Every time I cried and felt my Savior crying with me, my heart healed a bit more, because I was never alone in the pain. I would ask questions, and the Counselor would either reveal something new to my spirit or give me a Scripture as medication. I would talk to Him about my compulsions as they arose—wanting to run to substances or escapes—and He would pull me in closer, providing what I needed for immediate relief. Sometimes He would tell me that what I needed was to numb out in front of the TV, so we would curl up and watch television *together*. Sometimes I needed to eat something I adored, so I would bless a chocolate bar, and we'd eat a bit of it together. Sometimes I needed to sink into a bath and enjoy one glass of wine as I soaked in the tub and chatted with my Friend who had turned water into wine.

There weren't good or bad days—just hard and even harder days. But Jesus was so faithful to meet me exactly where I was, moving in close when I kept my heart in His able hands.

At one point, fear tried everything it could to invade my heart, longing for an invitation to stick around and move back into one of its old rooms. I'd be driving along, and a horrific thought would blast through my brain—scenes of Moses getting beheaded by a truck, or of me slicing off my fingers while chopping vegetables. Luke would leave for the store, and I'd get bombarded with thoughts of him getting held up at gunpoint or having a terrible wreck. A tornado siren would go off, and my entire body would freeze with anxiety.

Remember, *arguments* in 2 Corinthians 10:5 are thoughts that haven't yet become beliefs, and *strongholds* are beliefs that have rooted within the heart. In order to keep the fear as thoughts, I would immediately accept the reality of my fear, confess it, and get it out of my head and into the hands of Jesus:

"Of course my heart is producing thoughts of fear—I just got blindsided by death! Thank you, heart, for screaming so loudly that you need a Healer. I confess this fear and ask you to heal the source, my heart pulverized by trauma. Come on in, Jesus, and have your way. Love this fear out of my heart."

The more I accepted and confessed, the faster Jesus would get me back to a joyful connection with Him. Fear and bitterness were never able to take root within my heart as long as perfect love remained (1 John 4:18).

CHOOSING TO HEAL

You don't have to have experienced infant death, abuse, addiction, or depression like I did to live in constant communion with the Trinity, finding joy in every situation. Your heart must simply make the choice to *engage*, over and over again. Everything I have shared on our journey together can be applied to any circumstance, from the severely tragic messes to the places where you've hardened up to survive. As stated earlier, Ezekiel 11:19 says, "I will give them an undivided heart and put a new spirit in them; I will remove from them their heart of stone and give them a heart of flesh." No heart is beyond repair. No heart is too hard to soften. No heart is too far gone to piece back together.

Notice in this Scripture that it's *God* who makes the heart whole and puts the new spirit in, removing the hardness and making things soft. All He needs is a willing participant—and the choice to engage in this beautiful journey of transformation is entirely up to you. In order for your heart to be made whole, you must approach it with as much intentionality as if your physical body was diagnosed with cancer. You would do whatever the doctor told you to do if you were deathly ill—changing your diet, applying regular medicine, resting, and changing your lifestyle. If you really want your heart to heal and change, then you're going to have to treat it as if parts of it are poisoned by pain—in need of the medicine of heaven.

FINDING GOLD

As I have crawled out of bed every morning since suffering the sting of tragic death, my intention for each day is very different than it used to be. For decades, my goal was simply to avoid pain at all cost. I was surprised and angry at God when life threw me into the fire. But now, with unwanted tragedy a part of my reality, the pain pales in comparison to the Prince of Peace reigning within. The hell I experience is miraculously bearable when the kingdom of heaven is alive within my heart. At times, in the beginning of my grief process, I would question myself, wondering if I should feel guilty for the tangible peace that came so quickly after tragic death. But Jesus always smiled at this question, reminding me that this is how *He* lived—and He made the same peace available to all of us when we confess our fears, accept our feelings, and surrender them to Him.

As I have opened my heart wide to the Healer, I have been showered in His constant goodness and lavish love. Miracle after miracle continues to pour in as a result of the impact my Goldie's life has had on the world, proving that when the Lord told us early in the pregnancy that she would have a gift of healing, He was absolutely right about her destiny.

Luca Gold "Goldie" Gifford—our little treasure, anointed to heal the brokenhearted.

At her memorial service, my daddy stood up and quoted the most profound truth: "Luca's destiny isn't measured by her number of days on this earth—it's measured in the number of people impacted by her life."

And her short life has already impacted the nations.

Almost nine months from the day when she came into our world and changed it forever, my mom and dad were miraculously able to purchase a property for a healing center, naming it in her honor. *Gold Monarch Healing Center* is nestled away on twenty acres in the foothills outside of Abilene, Texas, and provides a haven of restoration and hope for those broken by the pain of life.

Each month as new guests arrive from countries all over

the world, we are humbled and honored to play a role in the lives of so many beautiful people. My powerhouse of a mom, my pastoral father, and our team teach each person practical tools for intimacy with God, while providing the space for their hearts to encounter Him, release trauma, and find healing. At the end of the day, our hands are just flesh and bone. We are just the facilitators that lead each broken heart to the Healer. But when we lead them to Jesus, miracle after miracle happens as they give Him the opportunity to dig deep to their roots of pain and draw each broken place back into His arms of love.

Thank you, Luca Gold, for your little life. Thank you, baby girl, for your strong presence on this earth. Every person who reads these pages and finds healing, or hears my words as I speak or write songs, every person who walks out of Gold Monarch Healing Center—each one has been impacted by the precious gift of your existence.

Thank you for teaching us to heal. Thank you for teaching us to thrive. Thank you for leading us to the Jesus who lives inside our hearts.

Mommy, Papa, Mosie, and Birdie miss you every day.

Until Father reunites us again.

"The Spirit of the Lord GOD is upon me,
  because the LORD has anointed me
  to bring good news to the poor;
  he has sent me to bind up the brokenhearted,
  to proclaim liberty to the captives,
  and the opening of the prison to those who are bound;
  to proclaim the year of the LORD's favor,

and the day of vengeance of our God;
to comfort all who mourn;
to grant to those who mourn in Zion—
to give them a beautiful headdress instead of ashes,
the oil of gladness instead of mourning,
the garment of praise instead of a faint spirit;
that they may be called oaks of righteousness,
the planting of the LORD, that he may be glorified."

(Isaiah 61:1–3 ESV)

Open-Heart Surgery

1. Jesus is looking at all of us, giving us permission to *feel*.
As the truth of your heart begins to surface and honest
emotions begin to bubble up, are you able to feel those
emotions *with Jesus?* Take a few moments and close your
eyes, once again being inside of your emotions with Jesus.
What does it feel like to be angry *with Jesus?* What does
it feel like to be sad *with Him?* If you're ashamed, He's
never ashamed, but He will comfort you and hold you
in the pain, whispering His truth to your heart. Quiet
the noises, get honest with yourself, and simply *be* with
your Savior.

2. Wholehearted living means being present in every
moment, no matter what the moment looks like. Can you
stay present today, alive in each moment? Notice details,
looking around you, staying present with connection
and relationship. Keep your smartphone off, turn the TV

down, and enter the reality of this moment. How do you feel in this moment? Can you keep your heart turned on in the present moments of each day?

3. Happiness is circumstantial, but joy is relational. You never leave relationship with the Trinity living inside of you. Have you lived to be happy instead of joyful? If the definition of joy is *someone is glad to be with me,* then take a moment and see Father inside of your heart, waiting with an enormous grin. He's waiting to commune with you in each moment, making joyful connection a daily reality. Take several minutes and meditate on this reality of constant connection.

4. Accepting where you are today *without shame* will change everything about your life. Take several moments, breathe in deeply, and practice the art of raw acceptance. No, you're not where you want to be, but you're safely surrounded and filled with Love. Yes, there are things about your life that need to change, but you're covered with empowering grace for the journey of transformation. Accept your heart, right now, in its present state, handing it over to Jesus. Through this relationship, your heart will be made whole.

Acknowledgments

Mom, you're my hero.

When your thirty-seven-year-old baby girl's heart was bleeding all over the place, you put your life on hold to pull my family close and help us heal. I've watched you pioneer inner healing my entire life, chasing after truth and freedom even when it cost you. You have been shunned, demeaned, and denied a title in ministry because of your gender, but you never let it stop you. My personal healing, every page of this book, and Gold Monarch Healing Center are all manifestations of your tenacity and longing to see the brokenhearted find wholeness. And though you still have no idea how big of a deal you are, and how desperately the world needs you, that's okay. I'll remind you, championing your greatness, until the day you leave this earth.

You and Daddy went far beyond what was required or expected in 2014, taking our entire family into your very home to help us grow and heal. Thank you from the bottom of my heart for being parents who are never satisfied with the status quo, always elevating towards greater connection and revelation.

Lucas Gifford, we both know that the wisdom that comes

out of me is a co-venture of a life lived with you. And though I might be the loud mouth that gets all the credit, everything I receive is also yours. You have the fullness of my honor, respect, and adoration as your wife, knowing I could never have become this woman without your care. Let's go change the world together, baby. I love you with every breath.

Kim and Skyler Smith, Kevin and Kelly Singleton, Darren Lau, Shane Stevens, Abner and Amanda Ramirez, Josh and Katie Hamilton, and both the Gifford and Black families—we didn't have to ask you to come. When Goldie died, you just showed up on our doorstep to hold us up as we walked through hell. There are still not enough words in my heart to adequately thank each of you for the greatest gift you could have ever given us.

Abilene, Texas, you loved us so gently after Goldie died. Thank you for taking us in and harboring our hearts during the worst storm of our lives.

Thank you, Jana Burson, for always believing in me, for working hard as my agent so these words can heal hearts all around the world, and for being the greatest encourager a girl could ever have in her corner. You're a gift!

Thanks to Carolyn McCready at Zondervan for being a kindred heart and for pulling in Traci Mullins to take my baby manuscript, delicately chop it up, and sew it back together to create the best version of this gorgeous quilt of a book.

Bible Versions

In addition to The Passion Translation, the following versions of the Bible are quoted in this book: